FAMOUS DEAD PEOPLE

AL CAPONE
AND HIS GANG

St. Louis de Montfort Catholic School
Fishers, IN

BY ALAN MACDONALD
ILLUSTRATED BY
PHILIP REEVE

SCHOLASTIC INC.

New York Toronto London Auckland Sydney
Mexico City New Delhi Hong Kong

ISBN 0-439-21124-7

12 11 10 9 8 7 6 5 4 3 2 1   0 1 2 3 4 5/0

Printed in the U.S.A.   40
First Scholastic printing, September 2000

CONTENTS

INTRODUCTION

Al Capone – Scarface. The greatest gangster of all time and famous as a BAD man. They'll tell you that he . . .

If you know about Al Capone from watching gangster movies, you'll know he was evil, ugly, rich, and ruthless. That he drove fast cars (50 miles an hour in those days) and smoked big cigars. But is that the real Al Capone – or just the legend?

For instance, they say Al was a villain. But did you know he lived with his mom all his life? Everybody knows that Al was nicknamed Scarface. But did you know he wore banana-colored suits and invented gangster style?

Everyone thinks of gangsters carrying their guns in violin cases. But did you know Al often didn't carry a gun at all, while one of his gang kept his shotgun in a golf bag!

Al Capone was the Big Guy. But he was even bigger than most people realize. A hero and a villain all rolled into one. In this book you can get the real story on Capone. Read his secret diary to find out what Al might have said about all those mob murders. Get the lowdown on roscoes, rubbernecks, and rotgut.[1] (By the end of this book you'll be talking like a member of the gang.) Turn to the pages of *The Chicago Bugle* to see how a newspaper might have reported the fights, the feuds, and the mob funerals. You'll also read Detective Lefty Lane's Gangster Files and have a chance to solve some crimes yourself.

Dust off your spats, leap into your limo, and hold on to your slouch hat. It's going to be a bumpy ride (especially for Al's enemies who all get bumped off).

1. If you spot gangster slang in **bold** or with an asterisk*, look at the end of the chapter and you'll find a translation.

PART 1: THE RISE OF AL CAPONE

YOUNG CAPONE

Slums, School days, and nasty Scars

AL'S SECRET DIARY

ALCATRAZ PRISON ISLAND   AUGUST 23, 1934

So finally it happens. This time I don't beat the rap.* They sling me in this stinking rathole on this stinking island for eight stinking years. I think I'll go crazy! know what? I shouldn't even be here. It's a frame-up. They're making me the goat* on account of my reputation. Al Capone. The papers say I'm the biggest gangster in America. know what? That's a loada bunk. Truth is, I'm the biggest in history. But Al ain't no criminal. All he ever did was help people. It's true — on my mamma's life! So how come I wind up here in this lousy rotten cell? Well, that's some story.

Forget about all them gangster movies. I can give ya the real picture. The rackets,* the parties, the raids, and the rubouts*...

7

Many people think Al Capone was Italian. It was a subject he was a little touchy about.

The *real* truth is that Al Capone was born in New York. It was Mom and Pop Caponi who were Italian. (The name Caponi is a dead giveaway.[1]) Al's pop, Gabriel Caponi, was no gangster. He was a poor but honest man (two things you could never say about his son). Gabriel was a barber in an Italian city called Naples. Teachers will often tell you Italy is shaped like a boot. If so Naples lies just where you'd scratch under your knee.

1. Later they changed their name to Capone because that's how Americans pronounced it.

Life in the slums of Naples was tough. It was noisy, dirty, and overcrowded. An English visitor in 1915 described it as, "more a pen of animals than a city of men," which must have made him pretty popular with the locals.

Gabriel knew he'd never get rich trimming the heads of hairy Neapolitans. Like many poor people he had big dreams. He'd read about a New World. A place where the streets were paved with gold. A land where the railroads were fast, the houses were tall, and anyone could become a millionaire. It was called America. Like many poor Europeans, Gabriel had caught the immigration bug. The symptoms were easy to recognize.

IMMIGRATION FEVER

1. THE PATIENT BECOMES RESTLESS

2. THEY DREAM ABOUT AMERICA

3. THE CONDITION BECOMES SERIOUS — THEY WITHDRAW ALL THEIR SAVINGS

4. GRIPPED BY THE FEVER THEY BUY A ONE-WAY TICKET AND BOARD A BOAT FOR NEW YORK

Poor Gabriel believed if he could just get to the land of opportunity he'd be sure to get rich quick. So in 1893 the Capones left the slums of Naples . . .

. . . and arrived in the slums of New York.

See the difference? The Capone family soon did. In Naples they were proud Italians. In New York they were sneered at as lazy immigrants.

THE LOWDOWN ON...
AWFUL IMMIGRATION

At the turn of the century every boat that steamed into New York brought more and more immigrants. The Italians, Irish, Jews, and Polish all had their own quarters in Brooklyn – one of the city's slums. If you walked through the streets of Brooklyn, the first thing you'd notice would be the awful smell. The salty stink of the sea, the stink of oil from the docks, the beery whiff from the bars, and the sweaty stench of overcrowded houses. Worst of all was the disgusting odor from the canal. In its murky brown waters you wouldn't just find rusty old barges but occasionally a dead body or two floating in the weeds. Sound like the sort of place you'd like to live? It's no surprise that in the mid-1890s more Italians went *back home* than came to America.

Yet still immigrants flocked in – drawn by fairytale stories of work and riches. In 1891 one American claimed 6.5 million immigrants had swarmed to America over the last 15 years. That was about one-tenth of the population of the United States. (He was forgetting that 95% of Americans could trace their roots back to "immigration" from another country.) If the new arrivals expected a warm welcome, they were disappointed. Some Americans had very fixed views. Italians like the Capones were regarded as lazy, stupid and, worse still, criminal.

One American writer claimed that Neapolitan immigrants were the worst. According to him they had:

Of course it suited some Americans to say immigrants were a cross between Quasimodo and Frankenstein. What better excuse to ship them back where they came from? The truth was that most immigrants' only crime was in being crazy enough to believe that America was a land of milk and honey. If Al Capone's family had stayed in Italy, his life might have turned out completely differently.

New York blues

Brooklyn certainly wasn't the paradise Gabriel Capone had dreamed of. Not only did it smell, people were jammed together like sardines in a can. There were no parks or trees. The district crawled with gambling dives, tattoo parlors, liquor stores, and pawnbrokers.[1] If the streets were ever paved with gold, someone had stolen the gold cobblestones long ago.

The Capone family moved into an apartment on Navy Street. The rent was about $4 a month. This wasn't much but then neither were the wages. The average wage was $10 a week – less than Gabriel earned back in Italy. For their rent the family got the no-extras deal – no heating, no hot water, and no bathroom. In the cold winters they huddled around the potbellied coal stove to keep warm. If you needed a bathroom, you had to walk to a wooden shack in the yard.

Gabriel and Teresa must have sometimes wished they'd never left Naples. But they'd only bought one-way tickets, so there was no going back. Gabriel soon opened a shop as "Capone the barber." His income didn't grow much but his family did.

The family had come to America with two sons –

1. Poor people gave their belongings to a pawnbroker in return for money. If they could ever afford it, they could buy their goods back later.

Vincenzo and Ralph. Before long there were seven more children. The family album must have had a lot of pages.

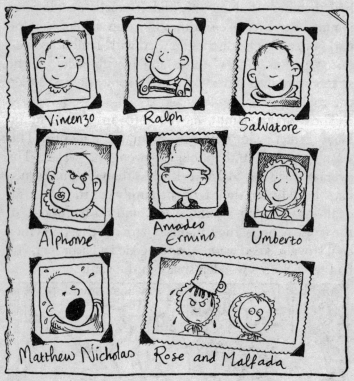

Baby-face Al

Alphonse was the fourth to come along, born on January 17, 1899. His parents had no idea that their little bundle of joy would grow up to be the most famous gangster in history. If they had, perhaps they'd have chosen a different name. Alphonse is hardly the name for a mean gangster. It's no wonder he liked to be called Al. Most of his brothers changed their names, too. Vincenzo later became James, Salvatore preferred

Frank, Umberto was Albert John, and Amadeo answered to either John or Mimi. Life must have been confusing.

Why did so many of the Capones have two names? Because they were Italian-Americans. Nowadays people are proud to say they're Italian-American or African-American but then things were different. Inside the house the Capones all spoke Italian to one another. (They had to because their mom never learned English.) Outside the family it was different. The children wanted to be accepted at school, so they spoke English and adopted American names. When he grew up, Al was fond of telling people:

> *I'm no foreigner. My parents were American-born and so was I.*

Of course half of this was a whopping lie, but who cared about the truth? Al sure didn't.

Al the kid

What turned Al the kid into a gangster? Did he watch too many gangster movies as a boy? Or did his mom take him shoplifting on Saturdays?

Neither. Gangster movies hadn't been invented and, as you know, Al's mom and pop were honest people. The Capones were an ordinary Italian-American family. Gabriel went to work in his barbershop while his wife looked after the kids. They were poor but they got by. Teresa sometimes earned extra money sewing and they took in a couple of lodgers (with nine children they hardly noticed the difference!). Maybe it was Brooklyn that gave Al a bad start. In the slums you had to be tough to survive. At school Al got called "snot-nose" or "Macaroni" by his Irish-American schoolmates. But he was big for his age and had a temper like a simmering volcano. Boys soon learned not to pick on Al Capone unless they were ready for a fight. Al was scared of no one.

AL'S SECRET DIARY

1909

After school I take a stroll down to the docks. I like it down there, the big boats loading up and the smell of the sea. If they're lucky, I let some of my pals come with me. We stand at the gate watching the naval marines changing the guard. It's a barrel of laughs. The big corporal, he's trying to lick the new recruits into shape. He has them marking time before they're allowed to fall out. If one guy's out of step, the whole troop has to keep marching till the lamebrain catches on. Today one sap is dumber than a sack of potatoes. He's out of step and the corporal has them all mark~~ing~~ time. Still the dummy doesn't get the message. I'm laughing like I'm gonna bust. So in the end I shout:

> Hey, number three. Get in step, ya big dumbbell! You're holdin' everybody up!

SAP

Dumbbell gets in step but his face is red as a ripe tomato. When he gets dismissed, the big goon comes steaming up to the gate and makes like he's gonna spit on me. Boy, did that make me mad!

"Oh, yeah? Step outside the gate, ya big creep!" I'm shouting. My pals are staring at me like I'm some kind of hero. And, when you think about it, I guess I am pretty tough. This guy's a six-foot U.S. marine and I'm only 10 years old. But who cares? I look 14 and I can handle myself pretty good. If the big dummy had just opened the gate, I'd have slugged him one, you betcha sweet life.

As we take our positions, the corporal arrives and yells at the recruit to get back to barracks. "You got his goat for sure, kid," he says to me. "But if he really spits on you I'll put him on report."

"Don't do no reporting," I told him. "Just let the big creep step outside the gate. I'll take care of him for ya."

Then I turn on my heels and swagger off. I can tell my pals are all looking at me and it feels pretty good. "You're crazy, Al," says Lucky. "You weren't really gonna fight him were ya?"

"Darn right, I'd take on the whole damn troop," I say.

Next day the story's all over the school – how Al Capone picked a fight with a U.S. marine.

Not bad for a 10-year-old kid, huh?

School for sluggers

Grandmas like to tell you that in their day naughty schoolkids got the cane. This wasn't true at Al Capone's school. Children weren't just caned – they were thumped, whacked, and battered! Fighting was an everyday part of school – and the teachers were as bad as the kids. A typical teacher was a brawny 16-year-old Irish girl. She'd be trained by nuns (who were former professional wrestlers themselves). Since the students were often just as big as the teacher, she kept order any way she could. Chalk and erasers flew like missiles. Rulers were used more for thwacking hands than for drawing lines.

It's no wonder Al often played hooky. In class he was an average pupil but he soon fell behind by staying away. When Al was 14, he was forced to repeat a year. Imagine the humiliation of sitting with younger children. That year Al made up his mind to quit school. As usual his explosive temper was to blame. Anyone who told young Al off was taking a risk and one day his class teacher pushed him over the edge. You can imagine what the principal might have written to Al's parents.

New York Public School No. 113

Dear Mr. and Mrs. Capone,

I write to inform you of a recent incident involving your son Alphonse. We all know Alphonse has a short temper but this time he's gone too far.

His teacher, Miss O'Hara, sometimes has occasion to give Alphonse a gentle slap on the ear. (When I say gentle, I mean that Alphonse is still conscious afterward.) But when this happened last week, your son flew into one of his rages. "Take your dirty hands off me!" he shouted.

Miss O'Hara says she only raised her hand a second time to scratch her head. But I regret to say your son then "slugged her in the mouth" (his own words). An ugly fight followed that ended with Miss O'Hara "taking a full count on the deck" (as Alphonse put it).

This school really cannot allow pupils to strike their teachers. I'm sure as caring parents you'll be glad to hear I gave Alphonse a sound thrashing. We last saw him running out of the school gates. He hasn't been back since and we've noticed the difference. The number of classroom fights this week has dropped to a mere 27. I believe all children deserve an education but in Alphonse's case I'm prepared to make an exception. So please do not think of sending him back to school. Maybe his talents would be better suited to a boxing club?

Yours sincerely

Edward T. Whackafeller.

Edward T. Whackafeller
Principal – Public School No. 113

P.S. Miss O'Hara comes out of hospital next week.

Al never did go back. At fourteen, he decided his schooldays were over. He'd never paid much attention in class – his lessons were learned out on the street. Once out of school, Al took a series of small-time jobs. He was a clerk in a candy store, then a pin setter in a bowling alley, and finally a paper cutter in a book bindery. But none of these jobs appealed to him. The truth was he was already moving toward a life of crime.

The streets of Brooklyn were teeming with criminal gangs. A tough guy like Al was bound to hook up with one sooner or later.

THE LOWDOWN ON...
GANG NAMES

What were the gangs of New York and Chicago like? They were more than just groups of thugs roaming the streets. The gangs of the 1820s–1920s were often the size of a private army.

Irish gangs generally fought with Italian gangs; Neapolitans (from Naples) hated Sicilians (from Sicily). Sometimes members of the same gang fell out with each other. That led to two gangs fighting over the same "turf." Gangs marked out their territory like alley cats. If another gang invaded their turf, it was a challenge to a fight.

Gang names were important. A gang called the South Side Softies wouldn't have lasted long. So gangs invented tough names for themselves.

THE SHIRT TAILS

WORE SHIRT TAILS OUTSIDE TROUSERS

THE PLUG UGLIES

WORE LEATHER 'PLUG' HAT TO PROTECT HEADS

THE DEAD RABBITS

GANGSTER SLANG FOR MEGA-TOUGH HOOD

THE WHYOS

SHOUTED "WHYO" WHEN GOING INTO BATTLE. WHO KNOWS WHYO?

Some gangs, like the Whyos, became so efficient that they even presented their clients with a printed price list. The "services" offered included:

	Punching	$2
	Giving two black eyes	$4
	Breaking nose and jaw	$10
	Jacking out (knocking out with a blackjack)	$15
	Chewing ear off	$15
	Breaking arm or leg	$19
	Shooting in leg	$25
	Stabbing	$25
	Doing the big job*	$100

Most of the gangs had their own junior following with members as young as eight years old. Gang life seemed glamorous and dangerous to a teenager like Al. At home he was cooped up in one flea-ridden room with his eight brothers and sisters. With the gang he was free to roam the streets and feel he was a somebody.

The gang was Al's way out of poverty. As one Italian-American newspaper writer said: "The Italian immigrant who did not become a criminal or go mad, was a saint."

22

Hanging with the gang

The gang that Al Capone joined in his teens was called the Five Pointers. The Five Pointers were the successors to the famous Whyos. In their heyday they boasted an army of 1,500 gang members terrorizing Manhattan.

Every gang had its headquarters. The notice on the door of the Five Pointers' hangout said:

THE NEW ENGLAND SOCIAL & DRAMATIC CLUB

Doesn't sound much like a gang hideout, does it? That was the idea. Most gangs disguised their headquarters with a respectable-looking "front." After a knifing or a shooting, the police would raid the New England club on suspicion, looking for the killers. But all they'd find inside were club members playing cards or checkers.

The police left red-faced while the killers made a quick exit through a back door.

Al's first jobs for the gang were small-time. A gangster called Frankie Yale gave him a job as a bartender and bouncer at a seedy bar called the Harvard Inn, kicking out awkward customers on to the street. Al was good at it, too. If you didn't want to be thrown out, his huge fists would help you on your way.

If things got really ugly, he was also handy with a gun. He'd spent hours shooting beer bottles in a basement to perfect his aim.

Scarface

Al learned about guns in the army. The First World War broke out when he was just fifteen. Three years later Al was drafted when America entered the war. Later he liked to boast to his pals that he got his ugly scars in a battle. Was it true? Not likely! Al didn't even make it as far as training camp. His famous scars were actually gained in a barroom brawl.

It happened like this. One night a bruiser called Frank Gallucio came to the Harvard Inn. Al made the mistake of insulting his sister. Frank pulled out a pocketknife and went after him. When the fight was over, Al was left with three ugly scars. One ran four inches all the way across his left cheek. From that day Al always turned his right side to the camera when he posed for a picture. Later it earned him the nickname Scarface. No one ever called him that to his face – not if they wanted to live long.

True love

Al's scars didn't improve his looks, but they didn't stop him finding true love. He met the girl at a party in a private club. She was tall and good-looking and her name was Mae.

Mae Coughlin was Irish-American and worked in a department store. Al was smitten with her and they married just before Christmas 1918.

Even their marriage certificate bore some of Al's little lies. It said that both bride and groom were 20 years old. In fact Al was only 19 and Mae was 21. He'd taken a year off Mae's age and given it to himself.

A year later Mae and Al had a baby boy. They called him Albert Francis. Albert was always known as Sonny (Capones never kept the names they were christened with, remember).

With Mae and Sonny to support, Al started to get restless. He wanted Mae to have furs and jewels, but you couldn't buy many diamonds on a bartender's wage of $25 a week. What's more, Al was up to his neck in trouble. People who wound up on his wrong side had a habit of coming to sticky ends.

AL'S SECRET DIARY

October 17, 1918

A big day for me. Know what? I rubbed out a guy today. No kidding! Al's a regular torpedo.*

So here's how it happens. I'm at this card game and I'm watching this kid. He's got all the aces and he can't stop winning. By the end he walks out with $1500. Well what can I do? I can't just let all that dough* walk out the door.

So I follow the kid downstairs and collar him in the lobby. "Hey, kid, who's holding the aces now?" I say.

He's looking down and I got my heater* poking right in his belly.

He says, "You oughta be ashamed doing this to me. I know who you are."

It was the wrong thing to say. What can I do? The sap's threatening to turn me in to the cops. So I give him the bad news.* BOOM! Pretty soon he ain't talking no more.

I stuff the dough in my pocket and beat it out the door.

Well, don't expect me to feel bad about it. The kid said the wrong thing. It was his own fault he got dusted off.*

Al got away with murder, but he already had his own **rap sheet** with the New York police.

NAME:	Alphonse (Al) Capone
ALIAS:	Al Brown, Snorky to his pals, or Scarface (but don't mention the last nickname, he's touchy)
HEIGHT:	Five feet ten and a half inches
TEMPER:	Nasty
FISTS:	Huge
SCARS:	Three on left cheek, jaw, and neck
RECORD:	Arrested for disorderly conduct (fighting). Discharged. Suspected of two murders.

By the age of 21, he had two murders under his belt and had put a third guy in hospital. Not only were the police looking for Al, so were the pals of the guy in hospital. New York was getting to be a dangerous place.

As luck would have it, there was a job vacancy elsewhere. Al got a call from a gangster boss called Johnny Torrio. Torrio wanted Al to come and work for him in Chicago. It was Al's first step on the road to fame and fortune.

GANGSTER SLANG

Gangsters used slang all the time – it was a way of showing you were one of **the mob**.

Think you could talk like a tough guy or make like a **moll**? Follow our guide to Gangster Slang throughout this book and you won't be no **fuzztail**.

rap sheet a criminal record

beating the rap avoiding a fine or a jail sentence

taking the rap what happens if you don't beat a rap

the goat a scapegoat – person who takes the blame unfairly

IT WAS HIM!

racket making money through organized crime

rubbing out, the big job killing someone

torpedo a hired killer

dough money

heater a gun

give the bad news, dust off to kill someone

the mob gangs, gangsters

moll a gangster's girl

fuzztail a creep

CAPONE IN CHICAGO

Blind pigs and bootleggers

Al was only 22 when he arrived in Chicago in 1921. It was an exciting time for him.

AL'S SECRET DIARY

September 28, 1921

What a break! Chicago is just the kind of city for a guy like me. It's big, it's loud, and it's fulla crooks. People say crime doesn't pay but in Chicago seems to me it pays pretty good.

I always knew I was cut out for bigger things. Sure I'm only working in a bar now, but you just wait. Someday soon the world's gonna hear from Al Capone. I got plans. And I don't mean opening no candy stores, neither.

Johnny's got a big operation going here and I aim to grab a piece of the cake.

Al can be a useful kinda guy to have around. I know what two and two makes and I know how to keep my mouth shut. I can handle myself, too. Sure, I might have to take care of*a few guys for Johnny, but that's life! (Or maybe that's death, ha ha!).

Anyways, I ain't gonna be running no errands forever. Al's got brains. He's too smart to stay at the bottom of the deck for long. Watch out Chicago!

THE LOWDOWN ON...
CHICAGO IN THE 1920s

- Second biggest city in America (after New York).
- One of the world's fastest-growing cities.
- Population in 1920: 2.7 million and rising – Americans, Poles, Irish, Russians, Germans, Swedes, Czechs, Bohemians, Italians . . . you name it, we got it.

- Area: 26 miles long, 14 miles wide. (We're talking BIG!)
- Visitors' comments:

"A dark smear under the sky."
British writer, H. G. Wells

"Having seen it, I urgently desire never to see it again."
British writer, Rudyard Kipling

"It's inhabited by savages. Its air is dirt."
More compliments from Mr. Kipling

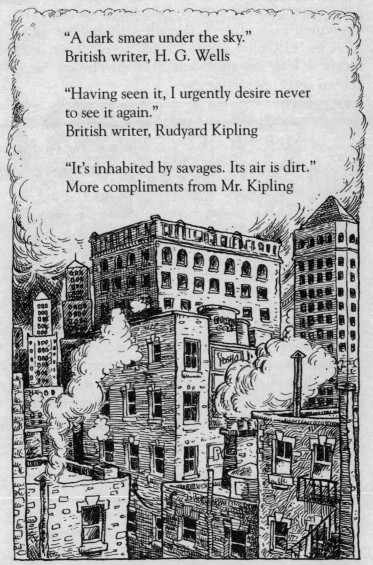

Chicago may not have appealed to snobby British writers, but it was a great place to be a gangster. It was rude, violent, smelly, dirty, and throbbing with life. The opportunities for crime were endless. During one single week in 1919, there were a record 250 robberies. That meant at least one bank or shop in the city was being robbed every hour of the day!

As one city alderman said: "Chicago is unique. It's the only completely corrupt city in America." Everyone in Chicago took bribes – from the police to the politicians to the judges. Even the mayor was as crooked as a three-dollar bill. Big Bill Thompson hadn't planned to become mayor. He'd only entered the election for a 50-dollar bet! But he soon saw that being mayor had its advantages. Big Bill turned a blind eye to gambling dens and gang rackets, as long as he took a cut of the profits himself.

Al Capone and Chicago were made for each other. Chicago was the crime center of America, and Al was to become its most famous crook.

Little and Large

Al's Chicago boss, Johnny Torrio, soon became his hero.

I looked on Johnny like my adviser and father.

Of course Torrio's advice wasn't the usual fatherly stuff about girls and shaving. He taught Al how to become a great crook!

Torrio's nickname was Little John. If Al looked down on him, it was mainly because he only came up to his chest. In other ways Al idolized the older man. The two of them became a famous double act, the Little and Large of crime. Little Johnny was cool, clever, and quiet; Big Al was young, loud, and hot-headed.

Torrio claimed he'd never fired a gun in his life. It was probably true. He always got one of his **hoodlums** to pull the trigger. (That way he kept out of prison.) He was the brains of the outfit, the criminal mastermind. He'd come to Chicago at the invitation of his uncle Big Jim Colosimo. By the time Al arrived in Chicago, Torrio was on his way to becoming a **bigshot**. He soon saw that his young pal could be useful. Al was more than just a big thug. He was a big thug with brains!

Al got a job at Torrio's saloon called the Four Deuces. Naturally the building wasn't just a saloon. Inside it had a few hidden features.

The Four Deuces

Before long Al got promotion. As the new manager of the Four Deuces the first thing he did was to give the saloon a respectable front. Al had learned from Torrio that a gangster shouldn't look like a crook. He should look like a respectable businessman. So Al had some business cards printed. They said:

ALPHONSE CAPONE
Secondhand Furniture Dealer
2222 South Wabash Avenue

To back up his story, Al stocked an old storefront with a piano, three tables, a rocking chair, some rugs, and an aquarium. A shelf of books included a family Bible. He even put himself in the phone book as an Antiques Dealer. But if anyone ever phoned up, a rough voice answered, "We ain't open today!"

The truth was Al was in a different line of trade. More accurately his business card should have said:

AL CAPONE
Undertaker
Funerals arranged for your friends

WE AIM TO PLEASE
2222 South Wabash Avenue

Big Jim and Little Johnny

Al's bosses, Big Jim Colosimo and his nephew Johnny Torrio, were doing nicely, thank you. Big Jim Colosimo ran one of the city's hottest nightclubs – Colosimo's Café. The rich and famous flocked to the doors to see the latest dances. A night at Colosimo's was a dazzling experience.

Moving smoothly among the tables was the host himself – Big Jim. Big Jim made other gangsters look cheap. He was fond of diamonds. So fond that that he wore them on his fingers, his belt buckle, tie pin, watch fob, shirt, and cuffs. If that wasn't enough he always

STAGE RISES AT THE TOUCH OF A BUTTON

GOLD CHANDELIERS

carried a bag of diamonds with him so he could play with his toys. Big Jim was making $50,000 a month from his business. But most of it was due to the business sense of his nephew Johnny Torrio. And Torrio was getting impatient. A golden opportunity had just dropped into his lap. It was called Prohibition.

The dumb liquor law

Prohibition – the law against selling alcohol – arrived in Chicago not long after Al Capone. What a stroke of luck for him! If the liquor law had never been passed, Al would never have become a multimillionaire.

THE CHICAGO BUGLE

January 17, 1920

AMERICA DRY AS SAHARA

"Last orders" were called across America at midnight last night. As Prohibition came in, booze was shown the door. It's now against the law to sell beer, whiskey, or any other strong drink. Supporters toasted the victory – with lemonade of course. But in American cities it raised few cheers. Before midnight Chicago's streets were busy with people having one (or two) for the road.

New Prohibition chief John F. Kramer promised, "This law will be obeyed in cities, large or small." Minutes after he spoke a truckload of whiskey was hijacked by a gang on Westland street, Chicago.

Loophole

Will the new law mean booze disappears down the drain in Chicago? This paper doubts it. The law says you can't make, sell, or transport liquor. But drinking isn't illegal. And it's the police who enforce the law. When did you last hear a Chicago cop turn down a drink?

Police welcome Prohibition

Perhaps the oddest result of Prohibition was that a soda-pop craze swept America. Men and women flocked to soda shops that sold milk shakes, marshmallow flips, and Coca-cola. Why the sudden craze? Rumor had it that milk shake wasn't the only drink you could buy at the counter.

Gold mine

In all the confusion, one set of people welcomed the new drink law with open arms. They were the crooks themselves! Johnny Torrio saw the new law as the answer to all his prayers. He could make a fortune from it. People still wanted to drink, so Torrio would sell them a drink – at a price. A glass of beer that had cost a nickel before the law, now fetched ten times as much (and was twice as weak).

Torrio was so sure Prohibition would make him rich, he was prepared to give Al Capone a cut of the deal. Al had already shown he was smart and was rapidly rising to become Torrio's business partner.

Only one thing stood in their way – the bulky shape of Big Jim Colosimo. Torrio's boss didn't want to expand into **bootlegging**. He'd recently fallen in love with a young singer called Dale Winter. The word had circulated: "Big Jim's gone soft." If Torrio was to build his liquor empire he needed Big Jim out of the way. Strangely enough, soon after, Big Jim was killed. Who shot him? Nobody knew.

Here's how Detective Lefty Lane might have described the mystery. See if you can work out who the killer was.

THE GANGSTER FILES

Case: Who killed Big Jim?
Date: May 12, 1920
Reporting Officer: Detective Lefty Lane

The dame in my office was the type who gets noticed. Slim, dark, skin like china and big blue eyes. She told me her name was Dale. You could see by her outfit Dale wasn't short of a dollar or two.

"I want you to find out who shot my husband," she said, dabbing her big blue peepers.

"Sure, lady," I said. "I'm a cop. That's my job. Who was your husband?"

"Big Jim." She let me chew on that for a while. I knew the name all right. Everyone in Chicago knew Big Jim. He was the kind of guy who had a lot of pals. A lot of enemies, too. I told her to pull up a chair and tell me the whole story.

Big Jim—
Dead as a
Doorknob.

Dale said she and Jim only got back from their honeymoon last week. (She looked about 19, and Jim was no spring chicken. Still, I didn't like to speak ill of the dead.) Yesterday Big Jim gets a call from his nephew Johnny Torrio. Not long after Jim has to go out on business. Dale doesn't know what kind of business – but you can bet it wasn't buying candy. Around four Big Jim left the house for an appointment at Colosimo's café. He had a red rose in his buttonhole and his pearl-handled revolver in his pocket. Dale said she kissed him good-bye. That's the last time she saw him alive. While she finished crying, I poured her a drink. She shook her head so I drank it myself.

Later I took a stroll down to his café. The rain was bouncing off the sidewalk like rubber balls. Inside the lobby I noticed a cracked window and a bullet lodged in the wall. I tripped over something on the carpet. Big Jim was lying face down. The bullet through his head suggested he wasn't taking a nap. From the angle of fire I figured the killer had been waiting in the cloakroom.

I grilled the doorman. Turns out a stranger flitted into the lobby soon after Jim arrived. Our boy was short, fat-faced, and wearing a

black derby hat. When I showed the doorman some **mug shots,** he paused at Frankie Yale.

Now there was a coincidence. Frankie Yale was Al Capone's old pal in Brooklyn. And who does

Frankie Yale – the man in the hat

Al work for these days? Johnny Torrio. It just so happens that the guy who stood to gain from Big Jim's death was Torrio. He gets the business, the whole setup. It was all starting to add up.

I stopped by Johnny's office to offer my condolences. When I mentioned Jim, his eyes filled up like a baby's. "Me and Jim? We was like brothers," he whined. It was touching. I was practically bawling myself.

We pulled Frankie Yale in for a **lineup**. But the doorman said it was the wrong guy. Dale never found out who left her a widow. Me? I could've taken a wild guess who pulled the job. What do you think?

The suspects:

1 Al Capone. 2 Johnny Torrio. 3 Frankie Yale.

Conclusion

I'd lay evens Al Capone set up the **hit** and Frankie Yale pulled the trigger. It all makes sense. Capone's boss Torrio wanted his uncle out of the way, so Capone made the arrangements. The killer had to be someone from out of town, so who better than Capone's old pal, Frankie? Torrio lured Colosimo to the café for four P.M. – Yale then did the rest. The doorman nearly spoiled the party. But he didn't have the nerve to identify Yale in a lineup. Can you blame the poor guy? As the only witness, he knew he'd never make it to the trial alive.

Big Jim's funeral was as large and showy as the man himself. Among the wreaths of flowers were two big ones. One said "from Johnny" and the other "from Al." It was typical of Capone. Whenever he had a rival **bumped off**, he always sent flowers to the funeral!

With Big Jim out of the way, Torrio was now lord of his own empire. By now Capone was his trusty number two. The barroom bouncer from Brooklyn had already come a long way. But he didn't plan to be a sidekick for ever. Al was watching and learning. One day he'd be a bigshot like Torrio, too. In fact he'd become the biggest shot of them all.

GANGSTER SLANG

take care of, bump off to kill someone

bigshot top gangster, leader of a mob

mobster, hoodlum, hood a gangster, one of the mob

bootlegger a dealer in illegal alcohol (named after the tall boots once used to smuggle bottles of whiskey)

rotgut, coffin varnish, busthead, belch, razors, horse liniment, tarantula juice, strike-me-dead, sheep-dip bootleg liquor — most beer and whiskey was watered down before it was sold to make it go farther (some of the worst bootleggers even used sulfuric acid to give their whiskey a kick!)

blind pig a store with a "blind" or blank front window — customers entered through the basement door and left with a bottle of bootleg liquor (alcohol)

mug shot photo of a criminal's mug (face) from police records

lineup police identity parade

hit a murder

AL'S EMPIRE

Beer wars and crooked votes

"Al? He's a good boy," said Teresa Capone. Of course, she was Al's mother so she would say that. But what was Al really like away from the bullets and the bootlegging? What did a gangster do when he got home and kicked off his spats? Like most Italians Al was a big family man. So he bought a big house on South Prairie Avenue to make room for his big family. Number 7244 looked just like the other houses on the street – a square, two-story brick building.

Inside it was a different matter. Al was now a rich man. He'd arrived and he wanted *everyone* to know about it.

Home sweet home – part 1

By night Al ran the shady Four Deuces and took care of Torrio's enemies, by day he was ordinary Al Brown at home with his family. And what a family! Life must have been tough for Mae. She was now part of the Capone clan. Al soon brought his mamma and his army of brothers and sisters to live with them. Poor Mae! At home everyone spoke Italian, so she didn't know what was being said in her own house. Maybe at times it was just as well.

THE LOWDOWN ON...
MARRIED TO THE MOB

In the 1920s women were taking a bigger role in life. They wanted to have a say in who ran the country, and in 1920 American women finally gained the vote. Other changes were happening, too. Women were wearing their hair shorter and had chucked out their stiff corsets. Women smoked and drank and began to invade the **speakeasies**. Some even learned to handle a pistol.

But things were different if you were married to the mob. Gangsters like Al Capone liked their wives to be soft, silent, and devoted.

> *The trouble with women today is their excitement over too many things outside the home. A woman's home and her children are her real happiness.*

Naturally it suited Al to think this way. While Mae was at home she had no idea what he was getting into! All her life Mae turned a blind eye to her husband's "work." As she once said . . .

> *The public has one idea of my husband and I have another.*

Mae's idea was to keep her eyes and ears shut.

She cooked, she looked after Sonny, and went to church on Sundays.

Gangsters liked their wives to be *respectable*. Johnny Torrio came home at six every night and waited for his wife, Anna, to bring his slippers. "My married life has been one long unclouded honeymoon," said Anna, not noticing the shady hoods who hung around her husband.

If gangsters were devils they wanted their wives to be angels. It helped them to fool themselves into thinking that – at heart – they were decent men.

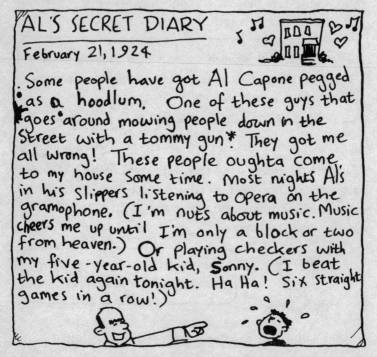

AL'S SECRET DIARY

February 21, 1924

Some people have got Al Capone pegged as a hoodlum. One of these guys that goes around mowing people down in the street with a tommy gun* They got me all wrong! These people oughta come to my house some time. Most nights Al's in his slippers listening to opera on the gramophone. (I'm nuts about music. Music cheers me up until I'm only a block or two from heaven.) Or playing checkers with my five-year-old kid, Sonny. (I beat the kid again tonight. Ha Ha! Six straight games in a row!)

Al Capone's a quiet, respectable guy. Ask anyone. He ain't out looking for trouble. He's in the kitchen cooking spaghetti. (I'm crazy about spaghetti and nobody cooks it like me.) Know what? I even wear an apron when I'm cooking. No kidding! Who wants to get sauce on a $12 silk shirt? Or take Christmas. I love Christmas. Know what I do then? **I** load up my Cadillac with presents and drive to my kid sister's school. Every kid in the school gets a present from Al Capone. The teachers too. That's the kind of guy Al is. A regular Santa Claus if you want the truth. People who say I'm in the mob don't know me. Al's just a nice, respectable guy trying to get along. They oughta get their facts right or **SHUT THEIR BIG MOUTHS.** Else someone might **SHUT IT FOR THEM.** Get the **PICTURE?**

The Great Beer War

Al's new house showed how far he'd come up in the world. As Johnny Torrio's number two he took half of the bootleg business – worth a cool $12 million a year. Torrio was right. Prohibition was a gold mine for any crook with a head for business. And at first there was enough business for everyone. Torrio made a deal that each gang would stick to its own turf. But it didn't last long. One gang was tired of playing second fiddle to Torrio and Capone.

The South Side O'Donnells were four rough, tough Irish brothers. The leader of the gang was Spike. Spike was a devout Catholic. That didn't stop him from killing anyone who got in his way. He sported polka-dot bow ties and cracked devil-may-care jokes. Ten times his enemies had tried to kill him. But somehow Spike always walked away. As he said: "Life with me is just one bullet after another. I've been shot at and missed so many times I've a notion to hire myself out as a professional target."

The Great Beer War broke out in 1923 between the dangerous O'Donnells and Torrio. At first it was just a price war like supermarkets fight today.

But the O' Donnells didn't stop at slashing prices. Spike and his brothers would waltz into a saloon with guns in their belts. They'd look the owner in the eye and tell him, "You buy your beer from us now – *or else*."

People knew what "or else" meant. It was the best sales talk in the business.

Soon the South Side O'Donnells were stealing business from other gangs. Something had to be done. As usual when there was trouble, Al Capone was the man to fix it. First the O'Donnells narrowly escaped an ambush in a bar. Then other members of their gang started to die mysteriously. Morrie Keane and Shorty Egan were truck drivers for the O'Donnells. They were taking beer to Chicago when they ran into an ambush.

Here's Detective Lefty Lane's report on the case.

THE GANGSTER FILES

Case: Get Shorty
Date: October 25, 1923
Reporting Officer: Detective Lefty Lane

Shorty Egan was no pal of mine. So when I heard someone had put him in hospital I wasn't rushing out to buy flowers. My chief wanted to know who tried to bump him off. These beer wars were starting to give Chicago a bad name.

I found Shorty in the east ward. He was wrapped in so many bandages he looked like the curse of the Mummy.

"How's tricks, Shorty?" I said, sitting on the bed.
"Just swell. How's it look?"
"I hear someone tried to take you on a **one-way ride**. Wanna tell me the story?"
Shorty's eyes flicked over me. As friendly as a lizard. He started to talk. I guess he didn't get too many visitors and he just liked to hear the sound of his own voice. "Me and Morrie, we got jumped by two guys," he said. "One of them's tall and skinny, the other's this fat guy. They trussed us up like turkeys and pushed us into the back of a car.

"Pretty soon the skinny one says to the fat guy, 'Where you gonna get rid of these **punks**?' The fat one laughs, 'I'll take care of that in a minute.' He's monkeying with his shotgun all the time. Pretty soon he points his gun at Morrie and lets him have it. A barrel in each side."

The lizard eyes flick at me again. "Morrie was a good guy."

I nod as if I care. "What happened next?"

"The fat guy turns to me. 'I guess you might as well get yours, too,' he says and shoots me in the side. Then he loads up again and gets me in the leg. He gives me the other barrel right on the **puss**. I slide to the floor. Then the fat guy climbs into the backseat and opens the door. We was doing about 50 miles an hour. He kicks Morrie's body out the door. I figure I'm next so when he drags me to the door I prepare to jump.

"He shoves and I land in a ditch by the road. I thought I'd never stop rolling. Must have passed out then. When I came to, I staggered down the road till I saw a light in a farmhouse. They called the hospital."

I lit up a cigarette. A nurse wagged a finger at me but I acted dumb. It was a good story but it lacked an ending. My chief wanted Shorty to name names. These guys had taken him for a one-way ride, bumped off his partner, and left him for dead in a ditch. He was sure to turn them in, wasn't he?

What do you think?

Conclusion:
Sorry no dice. The two hoods who **plugged** Shorty Egan that night never stood trial. Sure, Shorty knew who they were, but he wasn't telling. It's the gang code of honor. Never rat to the cops. Hoodlums lie, cheat, and kill all the time – but they never, ever tell tales. Now that would be dirty.

THE LOWDOWN ON...
MOBSTER MANNERS

Gangsters may have been mean killers but they had their own codes of conduct. Each gang had its own customs and native traditions. But some rules like "never blab to the cops" were an unwritten law for every self-respecting mobster.

1 WHEN A PAL OR AN ENEMY DIES, STOP SHAVING FOR A COUPLE OF DAYS. A DECENT STUBBLE IS THE GANGSTER WAY OF SHOWING RESPECT.

2 IT'S BAD MANNERS TO SHOOT YOUR ENEMY WHILE HE'S OUT WITH A WOMAN.

WAIT TILL SHE'S GONE, THEN SHOOT HIM.

BAP!

This code was sometimes taken to extremes. One Chicago gangster died while horseback riding. His stirrup broke and he was thrown and kicked to death by the horse. Soon after his pals hired the poor nag from the stables and took it to the scene of the accident. There they gave it a ceremonial bumping off, each gangster firing a shot. "We taught that goddam horse of yours a lesson," they told the owners.

One man was seen by eyewitnesses at several of the Beer War killings. His name was Al Capone. But guess what? No one was willing to identify him in court.

Spike O' Donnell was furious at the way his gang were being knocked off. "I can whip this bird Capone with bare fists any time he wants to step out and fight like a man," he said. But Capone was too clever to dirty his fists in a brawl these days. He had better ways to settle a score. Soon after, Spike's car was riddled with bullets. Amazingly the man with more lives than an alley cat walked away again. But this time he left town with his tail between his legs. The Great Beer Wars were over and the winner was Al Capone.

Vote for crooks!

In 1924 Johnny Torrio decided he deserved a holiday. He took his parents to Italy. Generous of him? Not really. While he was there Johnny did a bit of business, stashing $1 million in secret bank accounts in case of a rainy day. Business was doing nicely and he knew Al would mind the shop in his absence.

For the first time Al was in charge and he was eager to make his mark. He chose Cicero to be his first conquest.

Cicero was a suburb of Chicago with a population of 60,000 law-abiding citizens. By the time Al had finished, it would be the most crooked town in America.

Capone had an outrageous plan for conquering Cicero. He'd take over the town's government! Simple! All he needed was a puppet to stand for mayor so he could pull the strings. Al chose Joseph Klenha. Klenha had been mayor for six years, but he feared he was going to lose the next election. So he struck a dirty deal. Al agreed to get Klenha elected, if in return he got the whole of Cicero under his big thumb.

The scene was set for the most crooked election in American history. Imagine the headlines the next day.

THE CHICAGO BUGLE

April 2, 1924

IT'S A FIX!

Klenha and "talented musicians"

Chicago was rocked last night by claims that gun-happy gangsters took over an election. Opponents of victorious mayor Joseph Klenha are furious. They say the vote was a big fix. Klenha claims his opponents are just jealous. "It was a fair fight and the best man won," he told reporters. "I'd like to thank my election team for all their support. They're all talented musicians."

Thug patrol

Voters claim Cook County was more like Crook County yesterday. They described how an army of thugs patrolled the streets in black cars. The men wore slouch hats and carried machine guns. Many of them raided polling booths and threatened voters. Thirty-five-year-old Cissie Hopkins told us. "A man stuck a gun to my head. He asked me if I was voting for

Mr. Klenha. When I said 'no,' he grabbed my ballot paper and put the cross down himself. It was terrifying. Some of the voters were being bundled into the backs of cars. I don't think they were going shopping." But a Klenha spokesman denied there was any "funny business." Tony "Fingers" McGann said, "We were just there to see a **square deal**. Not everyone's **on the level**. Maybe they need a little reminder to do the right thing."

Voters get a reminder

Hospital case

Even before the election started tension was high. One of Klenha's opponents was rushed to hospital the night before. William Pflaum denied that he'd been beaten up. "It was just a dumb accident," he told reporters. "I walked into the door and blacked both my eyes, broke my arm, and three of my ribs."

Pflaum – unlucky accident

Many similar "accidents" took place during the most violent election in history. Forty people were wounded and four actually died. "People oughta be more careful," said Fingers McGann.

No Entry

At one polling station, ten "officials" waving tommy guns surrounded the building. Scores of people were turned away before they could vote. When the votes were counted, the result was a shock. Joseph Klenha had won by a huge majority.

The taking of Cicero was a triumph for Al. Only one event soured the victory. Al's brother Frank was gunned down in the street by the police. The cops claimed that Capone's brother drew his gun first.

> FRANK NEVER HURT A FLY. (SURE HE KILLED A FEW GUYS, BUT HE WAS FOND OF FLIES.)

A heartbroken Al didn't shave till the funeral was over. As a mark of respect he ordered the town saloons to close for two hours. It was the only time in Cicero you couldn't get a drink!

As for Joseph Klenha – he'd got what he wanted. He was mayor of Cicero. But Klenha didn't realize he was only Al's puppet. He soon got too big for his boots and started to ignore orders. Big-mouth Klenha even claimed he would run the gangsters out of town. Mayor or not – Al decided it was time to teach him a lesson. He went to the City Hall and summoned Klenha outside. Klenha came, bringing a policeman for protection. Al promptly knocked the mayor down the City Hall steps. What did the policeman do? Draw his gun? Arrest Capone? No, he quietly toddled off down the street, looking the other way. Klenha had just learned a lesson. He wasn't the real mayor of Cicero, Al Capone was.

Rolling in dough

When Torrio got back from Italy, he found things had changed. Al had got his first taste of real power and he liked it. What's more, the guys who worked for Al liked him. Take his personal chauffeur.

Bad news

Only one man in Cicero tried to resist Capone. His name was Robert St. John. St. John was the youngest editor of a newspaper in America. He was co-owner of the *Cicero Tribune*. Bravely – or stupidly – he dared to write anti-Capone stories. Al decided that one way or the other the newsman had to go.

AL'S SECRET DIARY

Monday April 11, 1924

Another lying report in the Tribune. Boy does it get my goat! They call Al a dirty gangster and say he's in the rackets. Me - dirty? A guy who puts on a clean shirt every day of the week?

I send a message to this editor guy, St. John. Tell him I'm sore. He sends one back saying he's sore, too — that I don't clear out and leave town. The fella's got a nerve, I'll say that. But if a guy don't take a friendly hint he'll have to learn the hard way.

Wednesday April 12, 1924

Ralph and the boys go over to give St. John my message. They take their guns and a cake of soap in a sock.[1] He ain't gonna be calling nobody dirty no more. Not after he's spent a week in hospital. Ralph says Mr. St. John got the message all right.

1. If you knew how to use it, a soap in a sock could kill a man without leaving a mark.

Thursday April 20, 1924

Stop by the hospital to pay St. John's bill. I know I'm too soft-hearted but that's the way I am. I don't like to kick a guy when he's down. If this St. John wants to play ball, we can all be pals together.

Got a call from the police chief. St. John wants to press charges against Ralph and the boys. Can you believe this guy? What a bullhead!

FRIDAY APRIL 21, 1924

St. John's outta the hospital. You shoulda seen his face when he stepped into the police chief's office. Wasn't expecting to see Al Capone there, that's for sure. I held out my hand. "You got me all wrong," I tell him. "Sure I got a racket. So's everybody. But I don't hurt nobody. Especially your newspaper boys. Hell, you give me free publicity. You guys write your stories and they get right on the front page. I get my advertising for free. Why should I get sore?"

St. John's listening but he ain't buying it. "Now this little trouble you and Ralph had," I say. "Too bad. Never should have happened." I tell them, "Let the kid alone." But they were boozed up. They forgot what I told them. They made a mistake and now I got to straighten it out.

As I'm talking I take out a roll of dough. I start peeling off a wad of hundreds. Four-five-six-seven. St. John is eyeing the cash in my hand. I think maybe he's gonna take it. Then, out of the blue, he walks out and slams the door behind him. I ask you, is that ~~dumb~~ dumb or is it dumb? You try to give a guy a break but he JUST DON'T WANNA BE HELPED!

As always Al had the last laugh. While St. John was in hospital Al bought the *Cicero Tribune*. How did he do it? By forging St. John's signature of course! The newsman finally had to admit defeat. He left town to run a newspaper somewhere safer.

THE LOWDOWN ON...
GANGSTER RACKETS

How did a crook like Capone become a millionaire who gave diamond belt buckles to his pals? Booze and gambling were his main businesses. But that wasn't the whole story. Capone soon worked out that the rackets were a quick way to get rich. What exactly is a racket? (You may think it's what you use to play tennis, but this was the 1920s.) A racket was the name for any crooked business that made money. There were different types but the protection racket was the simplest and most effective.

CHOOSE A BUSINESS-ICE-CREAM SELLING FOR INSTANCE

INVITE THE ICE-CREAM SELLERS TO JOIN YOUR UNION OR ASSOCIATION

CHARGE A LITTLE "PROTECTION MONEY" FOR EVERY ICE CREAM SOLD

LUIGI'S ICE-CREAM

The BANANA SPLIT UNION 'We visit every Sundae'

IF THEY DON'T, PAY UP ARRANGE A LITTLE "ACCIDENT"

OOPS

RASPBERRY RIPPLE

SOON ALL THE ICE CREAM PARLORS WILL WANT TO JOIN YOUR UNION

JOIN HERE

YOU'LL BE RICH ENOUGH TO EAT ALL THE ICE CREAM YOU WANT

During the 1920s, there were over 200 rackets in Chicago using unions and crooked business associations that bred like fleas on a dog. Even the elevator boys had a union with its own racket. If hotels refused to pay up, the elevators simply stopped, leaving hundreds of people stranded at the top of a skyscraper.

Most rackets went by respectable-sounding titles. The longer the title, the more crooked the racket.

NAME	TRANSLATION
THE SODA DISPENSERS' AND TABLE GIRLS' BROTHERHOOD	WAITRESSES
THE BREAD, CRACKER, YEAST, AND PIE WAGON DRIVERS' ASSOCIATION	TRUCK DRIVERS
THE JEWISH CHICKEN KILLERS	CHICKEN CHOPPERS
THE THEATER TICKET TAKERS' AND USHERS' UNION	KIDS WHO COLLECT TICKETS AT BASEBALL GAMES
THE SODA POP PEDDLERS	SOFT DRINK SELLERS
THE CHICAGO CANDY JOBBERS' ASSOCIATION	CANDY MAKERS

One of Al's favorite rackets was opening dog race tracks. The beauty of this racket was that the race was usually fixed. All you had to do was feed up seven of the eight runners with extra dog food before the race. Then the hungry dog won the race while the fat ones dawdled in behind.

Capone raked in the profits from everyone who gambled on his crooked races. But Al claimed his finest hour came in 1928. That was the year the delivery drivers of the *Chicago Tribune* were about to call a strike. Who was the only man in Chicago who could get the strike called off?

GANGSTER SLANG

pineapple a bomb (a Chicago election in 1928 was known as the Pineapple Primary – candidates were "persuaded" to stay at home by deliveries of pineapples through their windows)

speakeasy saloon or bar

tommy gun machine gun

one-way ride a ride where the passenger is not going to return – ever

punk a small-time crook or henchman

puss the face

sour puss a grouch

plug to shoot someone

square deal a fair agreement

on the square, on the level honest, straight-forward

stool pigeon a police informer

PART 2: THE REIGN OF AL CAPONE

CROWNING CAPONE

Funerals, flowers, and fancy suits

In 1924 Al Capone was the rising star in Torrio's gang. But Big Al still walked in the shadow of Little Johnny. A year later he'd become the king crook of Chicago. How did he do it?

There were two bigshots in Chicago. One was Little Johnny Torrio. The other was an Irish gang boss called Dion O'Banion. Next to them the other gangs were **small potatoes**.

Al's stroke of luck came when Torrio and O'Banion went to war.

Crazy O'Banion

O'Banion was a larger-than-life gangster. He walked with a limp because one leg was four inches shorter than the other. Not that anyone made fun of him. He carried three guns and could shoot with either hand. And his great love in life was, um . . . flowers.

Why would a mean mobster have a hobby like flower arranging? Remember flowers are for funerals. When a famous gangster died, every mobster in Chicago sent flowers. Dion ran his own flower shop, so every time another crook bit the dust, his cash register would start ringing.

O'Banion was part of the **syndicate** of gang leaders brought together by Johnny Torrio. Torrio argued there was enough business for everyone. ($30 million worth of beer was sold in Chicago every month, so you can see how well Prohibition was working!) Torrio's argument made sense, but the trouble was O'Banion didn't have much sense. He was as crazy as a loon.

Here are just a few of the stories told about him:
1. When he was at school Dion was a real daredevil. He had to be best at everything. When his classmates tried stilt-walking, Dion had to go on stilts higher than

anyone else. It earned him admiration – and a broken arm when he fell off.

2. One summer's day Dion was at his Malt House Brewery. Across the road he saw two police sergeants obviously keeping a watch on the illegal brewery. Instead of hiding from them Crazy O'Banion called them over. "It's too hot out here, come on in and have a glass of beer and talk it over," he shouted.

3. Another time O'Banion and his gang had been on a safecracking robbery. They might have got clean away if a watchman hadn't noticed them. At three in the morning, they were perched on a rubbish bin singing at the tops of their voices. Most burglars sneak silently away from the scene of the crime but not Crazy O'Banion.

Sooner or later a crazy like O'Banion was bound to upset the apple cart. Another gang in the Torrio/Capone syndicate were the Gennas. They were black-haired, black-eyed Sicilian brothers with names like Bloody Angelo and Mike the Devil.

You wouldn't have liked to meet them on a dark night. In fact you wouldn't have liked to meet them at all. The Gennas hated O'Banion and he hated them. It was all Capone could do to keep them from each other's throats. But maybe he didn't want to . . .

AL'S SECRET DIARY

November 4, 1924

Dion has to go. At the start he was getting along swell but now his head's too big for his hat and he's grabbing some of our booze racket in Chicago. Some chance!

He's spoiling it for everybody. Where we pay a cop a couple of hundred dollars, he slips them a thousand. What nerve! It's enough to make a guy wanna go straight!

Dion's nuts. He makes enemies. And them Sicilians, they hate him like the devil. Well, what can you do? It's a shame but they ain't listening to Al no more.

A few weeks back Dion hijacks a load of the Gennas' whiskey. Then last night he does something even dumber: insults Angelo Genna. No kidding! We're dividing up the week's takings

and I happen to mention Angelo lost big time at roulette last week. He's left an I.O.U. in the kitty for 30 big ones.*
"Whaddya say we tear it up?" I ask. "We're all gentlemen. Let's show some manners." Everyone agrees – except Dion. He just glares at me, mad as a pole cat. Next thing he limps over to the telephone and calls up Angelo. I hear him demanding to see the dough by the end of the week. It's an insult and Bloody Angelo, he ain't the forgiving type. Well it's Dion's funeral. Know what I mean?

Al was right. Within a few weeks Dion O'Banion had been shot. Had Al seen it in a crystal ball or was he mixed up in the murder? The police never got the killers. But maybe you can guess who did it?

THE GANGSTER FILES

Case: Flowers for O'Banion
Date: November 10, 1924
Reporting Officer: Detective Lefty Lane

Dion always loved roses. So I guess it's nice I found him lying in a window full of them. His mouth was open. His eyes were glassy. There were six bullets in his body. At a guess I'd say he was dead.

Dion died in his flower shop. Maybe that's the way he would've wanted it. But he left me with a headache. My chief wanted to know who made the hit. And I had a list of suspects as long as a wet Sunday.

I hung around Dion's flower shop looking for a lead. I found the delivery man sitting in the back of the store. A lean black guy called Bill. Bill didn't remember much. Till I put five bucks in his hand. That jogged his memory.

Seems Dion had come in about 10:30. He was expecting a busy day. A big funeral on Thursday. Around 11:30 three guys came into the shop to pick up a big order. Bill was sweeping the floor.

"You get a look at them?" I asked.

"Kind of."

I peeled off another **five-spot**.

"Two short guys," said Bill. "Black hair, dark eyes."

"Italian looking?"

"Kind of."

He grinned and held out his hand. (For a delivery man he sure knew how to make money.)

"The third one was taller. A smart kinda guy."

Bill heard the shots when he was out the back. By the time he ran in, the killers had made the street. He saw them jump into a car. As they made off west six cars swung out from the curb, blocking the traffic. It's a cute trick. Whoever planned the job had covered all the angles.

I pulled in all the usual suspects. Remember Frankie Yale, Capone's old hit-man pal from New York? We caught him boarding a train back home with a gun in his pocket. Naturally he had his story ready like all the others.

② Johnny Torrio-claims he and Dion were the best of buddies.

① Scarface Capone-was at home with his family

③ Frankie Yale-says he was having lunch with a pal.

Funny thing. The pal Yale says he had lunch with was one of the Genna gang. Just a coincidence? The world is full of them, ain't it? Who do you think killed Dion O'Banion?

Conclusion
Frankie Yale. I figure the other two hit-men were part of the Genna gang. Bloody Angelo got his revenge. Yale got paid. Capone got rid of a troublemaker. Everyone was happy. Well, everyone apart from Dion.

THE CHICAGO BUGLE

November 14, 1924

HATS OFF FOR THE FLOWER KING

Chicago came to a halt today – as a mark of respect for one of the city's meanest gangsters. Ten thousand people packed the streets to see Dion O'Banion's funeral. Flower-loving Dion needed 26 cars and trucks to carry the flowers for his own funeral!

Bystanders watched from office windows and rooftops as the milelong procession passed by. The gangster called "an arch criminal" by Chicago's Chief of Police was given a guard of honor by police officers! Mounted police had to clear the way so that the hearse could make its way through the mob.

For three days, Dion's body lay in state in a solid silver casket with angels at the head and feet. Ten candles held in solid gold candlesticks bathed the room in soft light. Filling the air was the perfume of a thousand flowers. "It was one of the most nauseating things I've ever seen in Chicago," said one court judge.

Wellwishers

The coffin was carried by the underworld's most wanted men – Hymie Weiss, Bugs Moran, Schemer Drucci, and trigger-happy Frank Gusenberg. Bringing up the rear were "wellwishers" including Johnny Torrio and Al Capone. An unshaven Capone told reporters, "I'm heartbroken. Who coulda done a terrible thing like this?"

Revenge threat

"Two Gun" Louis Alterie, a close friend of the deceased, said tearfully, "I have no idea who killed Dion but I'd die smiling if I had the chance to meet the guys who did – anytime, anyplace they like to mention."

O'Banion may be dead but it seems unlikely he'll rest in peace.

Police frisk mourner

Gang wars

Capone and Torrio were glad to be rid of Dion. But his murder didn't put an end to the trouble. Instead it set the stage for a gang war. The cozy arrangement of gangs working together and sharing the loot was over. From that day, Al was always looking over his shoulder. Over the next six years there would be a dozen attempts to kill him.

O'Banion's gang was taken over by "Hymie" Weiss. His real name was Earl Wajaciechowski. But most gangsters couldn't say, "Hey, Wajaciechowski!" so they just called him Hymie. Weiss's righthand man was Bugs Moran. Together Bugs and Hymie swore revenge on O'Banion's killers. Torrio and Capone were at the top of the list.

Torrio wasn't fond of being a moving target. He suddenly felt it was time to take a holiday. Al stuck around and nearly paid the price. A couple of months later, he was ambushed. Outside a restaurant Al's car was riddled with bullets from nose to tail. Luckily for Al he wasn't inside. But it was a warning. Al realized he needed protection. And as always he wanted protection that was bigger and better than anyone else had.

THE LOWDOWN ON... STAYING ALIVE

Most big gangsters went everywhere with a couple of gorillas. Not the kind you see in the zoo of course, these gorillas were personal bodyguards. After O'Banion's murder, Al Capone started to get nervous. He needed more than a couple of apes with violin cases. He needed *real* protection. Here are his top tips for staying alive.

1. "Two's company, but eight is safer."

Al never went anywhere alone. Even if he was just crossing the street his bodyguards stuck close. Al on the move looked like an armed football formation. He was flanked on each side by bodyguards two or three deep. His henchmen were carefully selected. They had to be big and plump so that bullets didn't get past them. Al didn't mind people getting shot, as long as it wasn't him.

OK BOYS— LET'S GO!

2. "Don't sit with strangers."
At nightclubs, strangers weren't allowed to sit at the table next to Al. It was the same at the opera. If Al was watching a show, his bodyguards sat on his left and right, behind and in front. It must have been bad luck if you were sitting behind them.

3. "Never show up on time."
Al never kept his appointments, not because he hated punctuality, but because it was too dangerous. If an enemy knew the time and place of a meeting, he could easily bump you off. Al made sure he was unpredictable. If he had a 4 o'clock rendezvous, he'd send a messenger at the last minute to change the time and the place.

4. "Bulletproof everything."
Even in the office of his HQ Al didn't feel safe. He worried that a gunman might sneak past his bodyguards and shoot him in the back. For protection he had a special swivel chair made. It had a high armor-plated back so bullets would bounce off.

5. "Be a night owl."
Some people like to get their beauty sleep at night. Not Al. (With a mug like his it was too late for beauty sleep.) Nighttime was when Al went to work. He knew that he was much safer under the cover of darkness.

6. "Travel by armored car."
Al had a car that even James Bond would have envied. It had so many gadgets it weighed almost as much as a Sherman tank. Al's car was a specially made Cadillac limo that cost him $30,000.

Al traveled by armored car even when he was just riding up the street. A scout on a motorbike would check the route ahead of him while a car packed with sharpshooters rode behind.

All in all it was easier to assassinate the President than Al Capone. But that didn't stop people trying. When Al tried to get life insurance in 1925, he found no company would touch him. It was hardly surprising. Most gangsters came to a sticky end sooner or later. Usually it was sooner. The next bigshot to have a date with death was Little Johnny Torrio.

Not-so-tough Torrio

Johnny Torrio was trembling in his little boots. He knew Hymie Weiss was out to get him so he hit on a brilliant plan. Where was the one place he'd be safe from Hymie Weiss? In jail of course. So on January 23, 1925, Torrio took an unheard of step for a gangster. He pleaded guilty to a crime!

Recently he'd been caught in a raid on a brewery. Torrio figured he'd spend a few months in a safe prison while Capone dealt with Hymie Weiss.

It was a brilliant plan except it overlooked one thing. Weiss wasn't the patient type. In the middle of his trial Torrio was gunned down outside his house by Weiss and Bugs Moran. Torrio was rushed to hospital with wounds in his face, arm, and body. By the time a weeping Capone arrived at his bedside, Torrio thought he was a goner.

What worried him most was the thought that his attackers had used the Sicilian death recipe. Maybe you've come across it?

Bullets à la Sicilian

1 Take three assassin's bullets

2 Boil them for five minutes in onion-water

3 Remove from the pan and rub well in garlic

4 Serve with a revolver while still hot

Why the garlic? It wasn't to ward off vampires. Gangsters believed that bullets rubbed in garlic caused gangrene. So if the victim didn't die of his wounds, he'd die of infection anyway. Nice, eh?

Torrio was convinced the garlic bullets would be the death of him – but was he right?

No, it was a load of bunk! Garlic doesn't spread infection any more than a brush with broccoli.

Amazingly Torrio survived his wounds. A few weeks later he appeared in court, looking pale and shaken. The judge sentence him to nine months in prison. Even there, Torrio didn't feel safe. He added bulletproof steel blinds to his cell and paid for extra guards to patrol the corridor.

Although he'd survived, he'd lost his nerve. A gangster's life was just too dangerous he decided.[1]

Soon after, Hymie Weiss got **iced**. He was crossing the street when somebody shot him from an upstairs window.

1. It was a wise decision. Torrio lived to the ripe age of 75. More than most gangsters!

Al had *no idea* who could have done it. But, strangely enough, it meant Chicago's three bigshots were all out of the way. Guess who was left?

Torrio handed over his criminal empire to Al Capone. That meant that most of Chicago was now controlled by one man. There were still plenty of gangs but most of them were in the Capone syndicate – which meant they took orders from Al.

Take a look at this map of Chicago in 1925. It shows the city divided into gang territories. Notice anything about Al's share?

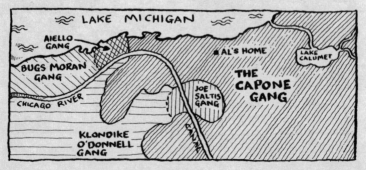

THE LOWDOWN ON...
GANGSTER FASHION

Al was becoming famous. On his first appearence in a newspaper his name was reported as Alfred Caponi. But now everyone in Chicago knew about Al Capone, and before long the world would know his name. It wasn't just that Al was ruthless and successful. He had something that other gangsters didn't have. In a word it was *style*.

Before Al, gangsters were hoods who lurked in the shadows. Why did they like the dark? Because they were fashion disasters, that's why! The old-style gangsters looked like cheap crooks. Robbery and blackmail was their line of business. They didn't pay much attention to clothes because they didn't want to be noticed. Al was different, he wanted the whole world to pay attention to him. And since he wore lime-green-, chocolate-, or tangerine-colored suits, he was pretty hard to miss.

Al had style, class, and lots of cash to spend. His shirts were silk and bore his initials – AC – on the sleeves and collars. On his nontrigger finger glittered a $50,000 diamond ring.

I MAY BE A CROOK BUT I AIN'T CHEAP!

OLD STYLE GANGSTER

UNSHAVEN FACE

FLAT CAP – PULLED DOWN TO HIDE FACE

CIGARETTE

WORN JACKET

CASH OR GUN BULGING IN POCKET

SCRUFFY BOOTS

DROOPY TROUSERS

Singlehandedly he invented the new gangster look, insisting that all his boys dressed like him. As one Capone gangster said:

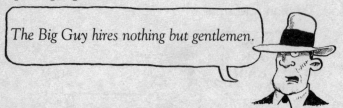

The Big Guy hires nothing but gentlemen.

Al's boys had to dress nice, say "sir" and work out in the gym twice a day to keep fit.

CAPONE STYLE GANGSTER

SHARP DOUBLE-BREASTED SUIT

PEARL GRAY FEDORA WITH BLACK BAND

CIGAR

WHITE SHIRT

VEST

WHITE FOLDED HANKY

DIAMOND-STUDDED BELT BUCKLE (IF YOU'RE ONE OF AL'S SPECIAL PALS)

SPATS

Al had class, he had style, he was **the berries**. He'd reached the top. Soon people didn't even bother to use his name. Gangsters just referred to him as the "Big Boy." Had all that spaghetti gone to his waistline? Probably, but "Big Boy" in gang-language meant Al was number one, the biggest wheel in the city. After all, no one was left to challenge him. Al was king of Chicago – but how long could he stay on top?

GANGSTER SLANG

small potatoes insignificant, small fry

tux tuxedo – formal suit

syndicate crooked business organization run by the mob

big ones money, a thousand dollars

five-spot five dollars

iced killed

the berries looking like a million dollars (a buck or a berry is a dollar)

rig suit

fleas and ants pants

village tux bulletproof vest

skivvies underwear

pinchers, stomps shoes

NICE GUY CAPONE

Fun, fame, and "no fighting please"

If they'd had TV talk shows in the 1920s, Al would have been first on the sofa.

MY GUEST TONIGHT IS RICH, POWERFUL, AND A LIVING LEGEND...

AIN'T YOU FORGETTING "HANDSOME?"

Al also had something that all gangsters tried to copy. It was known as "the Look." The Look was a silent, smoldering glare. You stared your victim out till he got so scared he'd do anything you wanted. The trick was to swell out your neck muscles and widen your eyes into a fixed, unblinking glare. The Look said, "Don't fool with me, pal – do as I say before I have to whack you." Young gangsters used to spend hours in front of the mirror practicing the Look. (Maybe you could try it on your mom or dad.)

Al didn't have to practice the Look. With his powerful body, thick neck, and cold eyes, he was a natural. As one witness said, Al could give off an air of menace while saying "please." A female reporter who interviewed Al was hypnotized by him (though he wasn't even using the Look):

Capone has dime-novel gangster eyes. Ice gray. Ice-cold. I could feel their threat. The stirring of the tiger.

Of course readers lapped up these thrilling reports. The newspapers couldn't get enough of Al. He became famous overnight. Now he was no longer just another hood – he was Al Capone, Bigshot. All the papers wanted Capone stories and Al was happy to oblige.

Al wasn't like other gangsters. Most criminals tried to keep a low profile. After all, rubbing people out wasn't a hobby you wanted to publicize. But Al *loved* the spotlight. No other gangster achieved world fame because no one was ever as big as Al.

It was a newsman who persuaded him to become a celeb. Harry Read was editor of *The Chicago Evening American*. He said to Capone: "Al, you're a prominent figure now. Why act like a hoodlum? Quit hiding. Be nice to people."

Up till then Al had always been shy of the cameras. In early press photos he looked like this:

But with his new policy of "being nice," Al started to pose for pictures.

In private Al was ruthless but in public he was a pussycat – when he wanted to be.

Al's sports album

Not only did Al talk to reporters, he started to go out more often. Al loved sports – so he began to appear at baseball games and boxing matches. Of course his bodyguards always went along, too. (Their favorite sport was shooting.) Al himself wasn't a great athlete. He didn't get much exercise as most of his life was spent hiding indoors. In his bathing suit you might have thought he looked, well . . . pudgy (though you'd have kept your thoughts to yourself).

Still, Al liked to play sport – and if he wasn't any good, he could always cheat.

Take a peek at Al's sports album. You might be surprised.

BASEBALL

Al was a keen baseball fan. His team were the Chicago Cubs and he was a regular at their home games. Once, Cubs' star Gabby Hartnett, autographed a baseball for Capone's kid, Sonny – or did he? There's a famous photo of Hartnett chatting with Al and Sonny.

But there's something wrong with the picture. The kid with Capone isn't Sonny. Al wasn't going to risk his beloved boy at a baseball game with 30,000 fans. So Sonny had a stand-in – a boy called Sam Pontarelli. Where was poor Sonny? Safe at home with his mom. There were drawbacks to being the son of Chicago's biggest gangster.

BOXING

This had obvious appeal for a gangster. It was simple, violent, and someone usually hit the deck. Even better it was actually against the law in parts of America. What more could Al want from a sport?

Boxing was part of the gangster underworld. One Chicago boxer, Barney Ross wrote that the biggest boxing fans were: "the gangsters on the one hand and the society crowd on the other. And whenever they met at parties . . . they got along like brothers under the skin. However the society people sometimes got drunk and nasty, but the gangsters were always gentlemen."

Naturally Al liked to bet on a fight. And naturally he liked to win his bets. So he used a fight promoter called Joe Glaser. Joe was such a good "promoter" he could see the future. He could tell you the names of the winners in advance and even which round would have the knockout! That's because most of the fights backed by gangsters were **barneys**. In other words the result was fixed. No wonder Al usually bet on the winner.

SWIMMING

Al always had a pool in his house and guests were welcome to go for a dip. Occasionally it led to problems. One night Al threw a party at his house for sportswriters. One of the reporters' wives decided to take a dip in the pool. In the women's changing room, she sat on a bench to take off her shoes. But she quickly leaped up again. Something sharp was sticking into her bottom. Lifting a cover, she saw what it was. Her screams brought Capone's henchmen running. What was under the bench? Just a hidden stash of machine guns, revolvers, and shotguns.

GOLF

Al liked to play a round of golf – but he was no Tiger Woods. His caddy, 12-year-old Tim Sullivan (more about him later) said: "He could drive the ball for half a mile but he always hooked it[1] and he couldn't putt for beans."

Al and his pals didn't play golf like other people. They brought hip flasks and drank from them regularly. You can bet it wasn't lemonade they were drinking either. By the time they reached the ninth hole, they could hardly see the ball. Pie-eyed and laughing, they dug up divots the size of ditches. Sometimes they paused to play leap frog or to wrestle one another to the ground.

1. In golf a hook is when your ball swerves off to your left – i.e., usually into the long grass or bushes.

Al made his own contribution to the game of golf. It was called Blind Robin. The rules were simple:

1. LIE BACK ON THE GRASS.

2. STICK YOUR FACE IN THE AIR.

3. BALANCE A GOLF BALL ON YOUR CHIN

4. SHUT YOUR EYES AND PRAY WHILE YOUR PALS TAKE A SWIPE.

When Al was the human tee, his pals put away their heavy drivers. They used their putters instead and swung *very gently*! (Clouting Capone's ugly mug was not a wise move.) Still, golf could be a dangerous game. Once Al was wounded on the course. Did an

assassin finally get him? No, he was picking up his golf bag when the gun inside went off. Al yelped with pain. He'd shot himself in the leg!

Playing golf with Al Capone was never dull. Tim Sullivan, his young caddy, had plenty of hair-raising stories to tell . . .

"A round with Al"

Often Al made up a foursome with his gangster pals. Once I was caddying for Greasy Thumb Guzik. On the sixth hole, he sliced his ball straight into a sand trap. I suggested a club to chip it out. Big mistake. Greasy Thumb took the club and swung at the ball. When it rolled back in the sand, he shot me a look of disgust. He swung again. Same result. The third time, same thing. Then he got real mad. He grabbed the driver like a bat and went for me, yelling every dirty name you could think of.

I ran zigzagging across the fairway. Luckily he was too fat and slow to catch me or I think he'd have killed me. He stopped finally, out of breath, broke the club across his knees, and threw it at me.

The next day Al is waiting for Greasy Thumb. "Whaddya mean treating the kid here like that?" he yelled at him. Greasy mumbled some lame excuse or other. Al then reminded him that he hadn't tipped me for yesterday. You can imagine how that went down! Grinding his teeth, Greasy got out his wallet and gave me one measly dollar bill. Al snatched the wallet off him. He pulled out $20 and handed it to me. Then he tossed the wallet back at Greasy's feet. The fat one picked it up and waddled away without a word.

I'll never forget the way Al stuck up for me that day. After that I began to help him with his golf. I would keep a couple of extra balls in the pocket of my pants. When Al lost a ball, I'd drop one near the spot where his disappeared and pretend I'd found it. He caught on pretty quick. He gave me a wink and said, "You're OK, kid."

Thanks a million

Al could afford a round of golf anytime he liked. By the mid-1920s, he was sitting comfortably. How comfortably? Well, try and imagine this. In 1928, his liquor and gambling rackets brought him around $100,000 a year. That sounds a lot, but you have to remember this was the 1920s. Today that figure would be $1,500,000 (one and a half million dollars)! Imagine earning that in just one year! No wonder Al threw bills around like confetti.

One story tells of him going to the can (toilet to you) at a party and dropping twenty-dollar bills on the floor like loose change. The attendant picked them up and stuffed them into his pockets. Afterward he said:

I pray to God he comes in here and pees every twenty minutes.

Al the peacemaker

Yes, things were going well for Al. He was rich, he was famous, and he was having a ball. There was only one small cloud on the horizon. There was always the danger that somebody might try to bump him off. Al was tired of all the gang killings. (Especially since he might be next.) He said he wanted peace. No, don't laugh, he really did.

He came up with a brilliant plan. He'd call a gangster's *peace conference*. Had he finally lost his marbles? Gangsters holding a peace conference sounds as likely as vampires becoming blood donors. But Al thought he could persuade his enemies to see sense.

Nine days after Hymie Weiss died, Capone called his peace powwow. The papers called it "The Robber Barons' Council." Who was invited? Most of the major crooks left in Chicago. Maybe you'd like to meet them.

The ROBBER BARONS

Greasy Thumb Guzik
Al's business manager and **bag-man**.
Why Greasy Thumb? The story goes he used to be a rotten waiter who always had his thumb in the soup.
Looks: Short-sighted, flabby walrus.
Special talents: Making huge piles of money, jiggling his fat cheeks.
Don't say: "Waiter, there's a thumb in my soup!"

Al "Scarface" Capone
The Big Boy, number-one crime overlord of Chicago.
Looks: Dressed to kill.
Special talents: Taking care of business, taking care of people.
Don't say: "Take care of my cat while I'm on vacation." You'll never see Felix again.

George "Bugs" Moran
Leader of O'Banion gang
Bugs? Did the guy have fleas? Don't be silly, bugs meant he was mean and mad. Let's face it anyone who tried to bump off Al had to be mad (or soon dead).
Looks: Smooth-shaven, baby face. But beware those temper tantrums!
Special talents: 1. Getting arrested.
2. Getting off the hook by bribery.
Don't mention: The last two leaders of his gang (both **pushing up the daisies**).

Vincent "Schemer" Drucci
No. 2 in Bugs' north-side gang
An arch-schemer? Er, not really. Drucci was always planning hare-brained robberies and kidnappings that wouldn't work. The nickname was a gang joke.
Special talents: One of his earliest "schemes" as a kid was stealing nickels from phone boxes (he was a wild and dangerous criminal even then).
Don't ask: "What are your plans right now?" You could be there a long time.

Klondike and Myles O'Donnell
Irish brothers running the North Side O'Donnell gang
Why Klondike? Nobody knew and he wasn't the kind of guy you asked.
Looks: Klondike – a red-faced potato, Myles – thin, fair, and sickly.
Special talents: Bootlegging, brawling, stealing Al's business (and dodging his bullets).
Don't confuse with: Spike O'Donnell. (No relation. Spike runs the South Side O'Donnells. Got it?)

The first-ever gangster peace conference was held on October 20, 1926. It's easy to imagine the mob of thugs meeting secretly in a smoky basement. But in fact there was nothing secret about the meeting. It took place in the Sherman Hotel – right opposite the offices of the Chief of Police! Al even had the nerve to ask a judge to be chairman. (Strangely enough the judge turned him down.) Reporters crowded outside the door waiting for news. One wrote: "Thieves, highwaymen, murderers, ex-convicts, thugs, and hoodlums . . . here they sat dividing Chicago into trade areas."

Al and his pals sat on one side of the table. Bugs and his gang on the other. Naturally Al did most of the talking. Some gangsters had trouble mumbling their own names, but big speeches were Al's speciality. He stood up and addressed the assembled crooks.

We're making a shooting gallery out of a great business. It's hard and dangerous work. When a fella works hard at any line of business, he wants to go home and forget it. He don't want to be afraid to sit near a window or open a door.

The thugs nodded their heads. None of them sat near windows. They lived their lives watching their backs (which isn't easy to do, you try it).

Al's peace proposals were passed without a murmur. Maybe someone took the minutes of the meeting that day. If so, they might have looked like this:

THE FIRST
GANGSTERS' PEACE CONFERENCE

Minutes of the Meeting

Present: A. Capone, B. Moran, S. Drucci, T. Lombardo . . . hey, you get the picture huh? All the ugly mugs in town.

Hymie Weiss sent his apologies. Being dead an' all.

Mister Chairman, Al, made an appeal for peace. There's plenty of business in the booze for everyone, he says. Where's the sense in rubbing out the competition? On a personal note, he's got a little kid at home. He don't want to be brought home one night looking like no Swiss cheese, fulla holes.

On a point of order, Bugs says he don't want no wise guys muscling in on his turf. A number of the guys took up the point. (Didn't get the next bit – lotta yelling and jabbing fingers going on around the table.)

Al – Mister Chairman – told everyone to shaddup and sit down. He passes around a treaty. (That's a smart word for the deal.)

Here's the lowdown:

Peace Treaty

1. All feuds to be buried six feet under – like the guys who started them.

2. No more beating up or bumping off guys from the other gang. Be nice.

3. No **ribbing**.

4. No muscling in on the other gang's turf. No muscling in on their customers, either. Let each gang make a dishonest living in peace.

5. Any wise guy who breaks the peace has to answer to their boss who should give him a little dose of discipline. If he ain't listening, **stiff** the guy.

Treaty was duly signed by Al, Bugs, and the rest of the gang.

Al proposed the meeting adjourn to the café to drink a toast.

Meeting ended about 2 A.M. Everybody best of pals.

The nice guys

The first gangster peace conference was a huge success. But the big question was, could it work? Could trigger-happy gangsters really stop killing one another? The answer was "yes." Well OK, "yes and no." Peace reigned in the city for 70 days. That may not sound like much, but for Chicago it was a record. In fact it was the longest period without a murder for seven years!

Of course someone had to go and spoil it. Al had made too many enemies to live in peace for long. So far he'd led a charmed life, but danger was waiting just around the corner.

GANGSTER SLANG

barney boxing match, a fight that was "fixed"

bag-man money man who looks after the cash bag

pushing up daisies dead

greaseball dirty

split case not to be trusted

scaly lousy

bum a tramp or beggar

one-eyed connolly nosy, an intruder

rubber sock timid

ribbing gossip (gangster gossip could kill – if a rumor started that one ganglord was cheating on another, someone usually ended up in the boot of a car)

to stiff to kill

KILLING CAPONE

Soup, silver nickels, and sunny Florida

Al had called for peace. But asking gangsters not to fight was like asking cows not to eat grass. It couldn't work. The man who broke the peace was Joey Aiello. Like the deadly Genna brothers, Joey was a Sicilian. He had eight brothers and a whole army of cousins. With a family like that he didn't need to recruit. Joey lived in a three-story mansion in a part of Chicago called Little Italy. His living room was covered with leather-bound books from floor to ceiling. Not that he was much of a reader – the books hid his secret store of guns and dynamite.

The War of the Sicilian Succession was the last throw of the dice for Al's enemies. Joey Aiello wanted to be boss of the Sicilian Union (a kind of trade union for crooks). But Capone made sure the job went to one of his pals instead. Aiello was furious. Joining forces with Bugs Moran, he decided to try and get rid of Capone for good. It was a dangerous time for Al. No doubt if he'd been keeping his secret diary, it would have made mention of it.

AL'S SECRET DIARY

September 17, 1927

That two-faced punk Joey Aiello! What nerve! Thinks he can put me on the spot.* ME - Al Capone! I'm the boss. I'm running the show in this town. That little rat better run for cover. Nobody puts a contract* out on Al Capone.

Word is, he's put a price on my head. Fifty big ones. **Only fifty!** It's an insult! I'm worth at least **ten times** that!

He hires four torpedoes from out of town. Tough guys with itchy trigger-fingers. Sicilians. Funny thing — they all wind up the same. Dead in a back alley with a silver nickel in their hand.

Who could have done a thing like that?   Beats me.

(Note — tell Machine Gun Jack not to leave his nickels lying around.)

October 24, 1927

Now he's getting me **real** mad.

Putting out a contract, that's one thing. Messing with my food, that's another. Tonight I'm eating out. My favorite restaurant, the Bella Napoli. Carlo the chef, he wants to see me. Says it can't wait until I finish my soup.

Carlo's scared. Last week he gets picked up by a couple of the Aiello gang. They say they gotta deal for him. The deal is either they bump him off or he agrees to poison me. **POISON me!** Those Sicilian skunks! I'm nearly choking on my soup. Carlo said he had to go along with them. They got a gun to his head and they meant business.

"I hope they paid ya well?" I ask.

"10,000 dollars, Mr Capone. Like you always tell me, I get the money up front."

"Smart Carlo. And how'd they want you to do the job?"

"Arsenic, Mr. Capone. In the minestrone"
I'm staring at my soup now. It's minestrone.
Suddenly I ain't feeling so good.
But Carlo, he's smiling. (Lucky for him!)
"The soup it's OK, Mr. Capone. You are my
best customer."
   That's when I get mad. I'm yelling now.
"Nobody, NOBODY tries to mess with Al's
minestrone and gets away with it!"
Better send for the flowers now. I got
a feeling Joey baby's gonna wind up
wearing concrete shoes.*

November 22, 1927

Joey's running scared. Getting
sloppy. He's got a machine-
gun nest in a front room at the Atlantic
Hotel. His boys are up there now. Waiting
for me to walk past so's they can
pump me full of lead.* But Al ain't dumb.
Now it's his turn to put the squeeze
on. When he's through, Joey
Aiello's gonna wish he'd poisoned his
own soup.

Al could have sent his boys around to start a gun battle.
But he had something better in mind. He phoned his
cop pals who went and arrested Joey Aiello. Joey was
taken to the Detective Bureau for questioning. Then
the master plan went into operation. It was Al's most
daring yet . . .

THE CHICAGO BUGLE

November 23, 1927

IT'S A RAID! RED-FACED COPS UNDER SIEGE

How big can a gangster get? No bigger than Al Capone that's for sure. Yesterday the man they call "Scarface'" pulled his biggest job. Normally it's the police who raid the gangsters. But this time Capone turned the tables. His thugs surrounded Chicago's own Detective Bureau in a mind-boggling show of gangster power.

Inside was the target – Joey Aiello, sworn enemy of Capone. Within an hour of Aiello's arrest, the siege had started. Sergeant Harry Roach works on the third floor. He told us, "I heard a squeal of brakes and looked out the window. A fleet of cabs were pulling up. Out jump about twenty guys packing machine guns and automatics. At first I thought they were cops but instead of coming in, they scattered all around the building. That was when I got it. These guys weren't cops, they were Capone's crooks. They had the darn nerve to hold up a police station!"

Police take action

Cellmates

Armed detectives collared one of Capone's gang outside the main door. But they blundered when they threw Louis Campagna in a cell. Next door was Joey Aiello. Police only helped Capone to deliver his deadly message. Campagna told the terrified Aiello he'd never make it down the street alive. Police Chief O'Connor said Aiello begged him for protection. "He was shaking like a leaf," said O'Connor. "I promised him protection all right – all the way back to Italy." Friends said Aiello and his family had left town last night. The odds are he won't be back.

Aiello – left town in a hurry

The Boss

At a press conference, Capone told reporters. "I'm the boss. Don't let anybody kid you into thinking I can be run out of town."

Chicago's police force wouldn't dream of it. This morning they're too busy wiping the egg off their faces.

Bye-bye Chicago

Al was at the height of his fame and power. All over America he hit the headlines. Law-abiding citizens read the papers and were shocked.

In Chicago Capone's power was starting to look embarrassing. It was OK for the ganglord to be bribing cops *in private*. But it wasn't OK when he made the police look like idiots *in public*. Big Bill Thompson, mayor of Chicago, had plans to run for President.

Naturally, having America's number-one crook in his city didn't look too good. Big Bill started to crack down on Capone's rackets.

How did Al react? By saying he was leaving Chicago.

Al held another press conference before he left. It was one of his best. Al was always a terrific liar. He could have lied for America in the Olympics. But even by his standards, this was a triumph. Here is just a sample of the whoppers he told:

> *I have never been convicted of a crime nor have I ever directed anyone else to commit a crime.*
>
> *I don't pose as a plaster saint, but I never killed anyone. I never stuck up a man in my life. Neither did any of my agents rob anybody or burglarize any homes while they worked for me. They might have pulled plenty of jobs before they came with me but not while they were in my outfit.*

Al left Chicago before Christmas 1927. He left with "gratitude to my friends and forgiveness for my enemies" (and if you believe that, see a doctor). He didn't know when he'd be back. But he'd overlooked one thing. If Chicago – gangster city – didn't want Al Capone, nowhere else did, either. Al soon became known as "The Man Without a Country." Wherever he went, he was turned away.

Dear Mom

Los Angeles is a swell city. Fulla movie stars. Today I take a tour of a movie studio. That's a swell racket. A real peach. Making millions of bucks just goofing around in front of a camera. Maybe they'll make a movie outta my life one day. Call it "Al Capone - the Hero of the Century!:" I even got an idea who could play the starring role. (But you know how modest I am.)

Everything's going swell till some cop arrives to break up the party. Says a lowlife creep ain't wanted in California. He's personally come to run me outta town. (I coulda slipped the guy a few hundred bucks, but maybe the cops ain't touchable* here.)

It's pretty tough when a guy can't take a little vacation in peace. I'm

> just a tourist. I gotta pile of cash to spend. Whoever heard of running a guy outta town just for spending money, huh?
>
> Catching the next train home to Chicago. Don't tell the cops or they'll want to throw a welcome party.
>
> Your loving son Al xxxxx

Al was right. The cops were waiting for him. Six shotguns were trained on him as he stepped from the train. He spent a night in jail for carrying concealed weapons.

IF THEY'D JUST ASKED, I'D HAVE LET THEM HAVE IT

Son of Al

Al found himself a prisoner in his own home. Whenever he went out the cops followed him. Life was tough. But what was it like for his family? By this time Al's little boy, Sonny, was nine. You might imagine it'd be thrilling to have a famous gangster for a dad. But Sonny just longed for a normal life like his schoolfriends.

He was a shy, quiet boy who had to wear a hearing aid. Al doted on his beloved boy and worried constantly that someone might try to kidnap him. As a result poor Sonny hardly went out of the house.

Being the son of Al Capone was no joke. Take a peek at Sonny's photo album and you'll get the picture.

Softball game - bookies v.s. Pops team. That's me dropping the ball.

Party at our house. Seventy-five kids from my school came. Pop served cake and candy and balloons. Maybe I'll have some friends now

Waving good-bye to Pop as he goes off on vacation.

During this period Sonny probably saw more of his dad than usual. Often Al used to stay away from home for weeks or months at a time. But now he was almost under house arrest. What he needed was a hideaway so he could lie low until the fuss blew over.

This time he tried sunny Miami, Florida. Miami didn't want America's biggest gangster, but it didn't mind taking his money. Once again Al found himself hunted – this time by estate agents.

Home sweet home – Part 2

Al finally settled on his dream home on Palm Island. It was a man-made island, fringed by palm trees and overlooking the bay. Al's Spanish-style villa had the word *millionaire* written all over it.

Al's Miami paradise cost him $140,000 (over $1 million in today's money). The alterations kept an army of architects, carpenters, and builders busy for months. What Al wanted most was privacy. No sign on the door said "Keep out," but one look at Al's home and you got the message. It was like a fortified castle.

In his Miami paradise, Al, the poor kid from Brooklyn, felt he'd finally arrived. He had a lifesize oil painting of the Capone family in his living room. At the foot of his four-poster bed he kept his loot stashed in a money chest. "Never trust a bank" was Al's motto – you never knew when some crook might try to rob it.

When his pals came to visit, Al liked to show off. Packing a picnic of salami sandwiches and beer, he'd hire a seaplane to fly them to the beach. To relax he sat on the dock in his bathrobe, fishing and puffing on a fat cigar. Sometimes he fed breadcrumbs to the tropical fish with his dear Sonny.

Al spent his winters in the Florida sunshine. In summer he returned to Chicago and in 1928 he moved his Chicago HQ to the Lexington Hotel. Now he had two safe houses – as well as his home on Prairie Avenue. The Lexington had ten floors. Al and his "staff" took up two of them.

Al's private chef cooked his meals, making sure to taste each dish before serving. (Just in case anyone tried to mess with the minestrone.) The Lexington was perfect for Al. That was where he ran his business, so that Mae never really knew what he was up to. The hotel also hid a secret within its walls. It was Al's hidden escape route. This is how it worked:

① DOWNSTAIRS, A LOOKOUT SOUNDS THE ALARM

② AL MAKES A QUICK EXIT WITH HIS BODYGUARDS

③ HE TAKES A FREIGHT ELEVATOR TO THE SECOND FLOOR

④ SLIPS INTO A MAIDS' CHANGING ROOM

⑤ A FULL-LENGTH MIRROR SWINGS BACK TO REVEAL...

...A SECRET DOOR

⑥ AL SLINKS THROUGH THE HOTEL OFFICE AND DOWN TWO FLIGHTS OF STAIRS

⑦ HIS CAR'S WAITING AT A SIDE ENTRANCE. AL MELTS INTO THE NIGHT

... LEAVING BAFFLED COPS TO SEARCH HIS EMPTY ROOMS.

Top of the ops

When he wasn't tending to business in Chicago, Al liked to relax with a spot of music.

Growing up in Brooklyn he had learned to love opera from Signor Tutino Giovanni, Dramatic Tenor. How did little Al afford to go to the opera? He didn't. Signor Giovanni was an organ grinder who sang in the street. Al's love of opera stayed with him all his life. When he grew up he bought every record by Enrico Caruso, the famous tenor. Al played them on the gramophone, listening for hours on end. It's easy to see why Al would like opera – it's big, bold, and larger than life. What's more, its characters often come to a sticky end.

JUST LIKE REAL LIFE!

All that Jazz

Opera was tops for Al, but jazz came a close second. Jazz was the pop music of the 1920s and Chicago danced to its beat. Big names like Louis Armstrong, Jelly Roll Morton, and Duke Ellington came to town.

Playing Chicago could be a scary experience, as the famous Fats Waller discovered. Fats was a hot singer and pianist known as the "harmful little armful." One night he was leaving a concert when he was kidnapped. Four gun-toting thugs bundled him into the back of a limo. The car sped off into the night. In the backseat Fats was sweating. Being kidnapped by four mean-looking hoodlums usually meant one thing. Fats figured he'd tinkled his last tune.

The limo headed for Cicero and pulled up at the Hawthorne Inn. Inside Fats found a party already in progress. The hoods pushed him to a piano and ordered him to play. Gradually it dawned on Fats that he wasn't going to die. He'd come to a birthday party for Al Capone. What's more, he was the surprise present. Grateful to be alive, Fats played on – and on. Al brought him champagne and stuffed his pockets with dollar bills.

The crime king knew how to throw a party. This one lasted for THREE DAYS!

At the end Fats Waller went home, drunk, exhausted, and with thousands of dollars in his pockets.

At another party, Al turned into a musician himself. The band that night belonged to composer Jule Styne. Capone had asked if he could conduct one number. It was his favorite: *Rhapsody in Blue* by George Gershwin. Swapping his gun for a conductor's baton, he waved his plump arms and the band started to play. Styne said afterwards, "He wasn't in time, but all his life it must have been something he'd wanted to do. By the end of the number he had tears in his eyes."

"Music soothes the savage beast" wrote William Shakespeare. In Capone it also brought out his wallet. That night he gave everyone in the band $100.

Running out of time

Soon it would be time for Al to face the music himself. So far he'd outwitted all his enemies. The gangs couldn't kill him and the government couldn't arrest him. But maybe he was getting *too* big-headed. The following year, 1929, Al went too far. The world was stunned by an event so grisly, it shocked even the gangsters. St. Valentine's Day had always been a day for kisses and cards. In Chicago it was about to become known for something else . . .

The St. Valentine's Day Massacre is the most famous gangster crime in history. Of course there had been gang murders before in Chicago. (They came along as regularly as a bus.) But this murder was something different. Not only was it more shocking – it also posed a mystery. No one ever knew for certain who did it. Though of course, one name was suspected. These are the facts, see if you can work it out.

THE GANGSTER FILES

Case: St. Valentine's Day Greetings
Date: February 14, 1929
Reporting Officer: Detective Lefty Lane

Me, I ain't the mushy type. Hearts and flowers, moonlight and romance – you can keep 'em, sister. So it's no surprise I wasn't sending out cards on Valentine's Day. But someone sure was. The kind of card that carries a death wish inside. Seven of the Moran mob got the message.

St. Valentine's Day was a cold one. My office was so cold even the cockroaches were wearing snowshoes. Around eleven, I got a call about the bodies in the garage on Clarkson Street. Now I know this is Chicago, but seven bodies? That's not a murder, that's a war zone!

When I got to the scene, it wasn't a pretty picture. Blood on the walls. The bodies were sprawled out on the deck.

And you wanna know the funny part? They were shot in the back. Not one of them had drawn his gun. Why would seven mean hoodlums turn their backs and face a wall without a fight?

Bugs Moran himself wasn't one of them (not that I was about to throw a party). Way it looked, they were lined up against the wall, hands in the air. They weren't expecting no funny stuff. Someone got the jump on them.

One guy was still breathing. I took a closer look. It was Frankie Gusenburg, the muscle in the Moran outfit.

"Who did it, Frankie?" I asked. "Who shot you?"

"Nobody shot me," he croaked. (The same old gangster line. Boy, you'd think they'd get sick if it.) He wouldn't squeal. They took him to the hospital. (It breaks my heart but Frankie didn't make it.)

I grilled the neighbors. A dame across the street had seen two uniform cops arrive. Later they left the garage taking two hoods to the car at gunpoint.

It didn't add up. If it was an arrest, who were the two cops? No one had been called to Clarkson

Street this morning. Unless . . . My brain cranked into gear. Unless the cops weren't real cops. What if the Moran mob walked into a trap? The phoney cops lined them against the wall, then their pals walked in with tommy guns and pumped them full of lead.

As they left maybe the "cops" pretended to arrest their pals to throw any witnesses off the scent.

It was a good theory. But it didn't tell me who the killers were. Back at my office I watched the cockroaches moving out and ran through the suspects.

No prizes for guessing the prime suspect . . .

Suspect No. 1 – Al Capone. The Big Boy had the motive. Everyone knows Scarface and Bugs weren't exactly sweethearts. Mighty convenient for Al if half the Moran mob did a disappearing act. Only one problem with pinning the murder on him – Capone's sunning himself in Florida right now. Claims he was on the phone to the Miami District Attorney at the very hour of the murder. Now there's a lucky coincidence.

Suspect No. 2 – "Machine-Gun" Jack McGurn. Jack's the hit man in Capone's operation. He could have planned a job like this, with or without the Big Boy. McGurn was even picked out by a witness. Snag is he's got an alibi. She's blonde and beautiful. What's more she swears Jack was at a hotel with her at the time of the shooting.

Suspect No. 3 – Crooked cops. What if cops did make the hit? Witnesses saw two cops arrive and go into the garage. They even had a squad car. Maybe they were bad cops who had some **beef** against the Moran mob. What if Bugs hadn't paid up some **hush money** he owed them? Still, mowing down seven guys in cold blood – would any cop do that? You tell me.

St. Valentine's Day. Who needs it? And who needs a crime like this one – with seven stiffs and no one to take the rap? I don't need to tell you the case was never solved. This is Chicago. Seven guys shot in broad daylight, but no one can **finger** the killers. So that's the story. Who do you suspect?

Conclusion

In the words of Bugs Moran, "Only Capone kills like that." I figure Bugs was right. Only Capone was smart enough to have planned an operation like that. Ask yourself – why was Capone in Miami at the time? Why did he stop making calls to Chicago a few days before the killings? Capone made sure he was clean. Too clean if you ask me.

Machine-Gun Jack's story was that he spent the morning with his girl, Louise Rolfe. When the heat was on Jack and Louise announced they'd got married. Why the sudden urge to get a licence? The law says a wife can't give evidence against her husband in court. I told you Jack was smart.

As for Bugs Moran, it was a stroke of pure luck saved his life. He arrived late at the garage and saw the police car. Instead of going inside, he decided to take a walk till the coast was clear.

The St. Valentine's Day Massacre rid Al of the last big rival gang. Bugs Moran might still vow revenge on Capone, but his gang was broken. Al Capone should have been sitting pretty. But the truth was that the savage killing backfired. St. Valentine's was the day the world turned against Al Capone for good. Before the massacre Al was known as a famous outlaw, now he was known as a famous killer. The government couldn't let him get away with it much longer. It was time to nail Capone once and for all.

GANGSTER SLANG

on the spot marked for death

contract most contracts are for doing a job – a mob contract was the same, except in this case the job was killing someone

concrete shoes a weight attached to the victim's feet to make sure he sank to the bottom of the river

pump full of lead, tattoo to riddle with bullets

beef a complaint

hush money a bribe to keep your mouth shut

to finger to accuse of a crime

sob sister a reporter who writes about deaths and funerals

touchable, right cop a cop who takes bribes

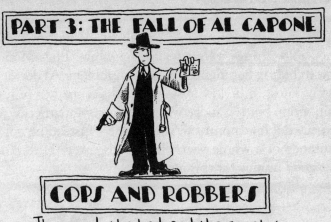

PART 3: THE FALL OF AL CAPONE

COPS AND ROBBERS

The good, the bad, and the sneaky

The St. Valentine's Day Massacre made headlines all over the world. And Al Capone's name was mentioned in every report. What did he do? Lie low for a while and keep his mouth shut? Are you kidding? He lapped up all the attention he was getting! In Florida he invited reporters and gossip writers for cosy chats at his villa. It never occurred to him that this might be a bad idea. In the past Al's crimes had caused red faces in Chicago, but now he was a national scandal that wouldn't go away. Something had to be done. Even Herbert Hoover – the President of the United States – vowed to put Al behind bars.

Hoover got his wish. But not the way he'd imagined. For the first time in his life, Al *wanted* to go to jail. He even paid two detectives to arrest him! It happened on May 17 outside a cinema in Atlantic City. Al's crime was carrying a concealed weapon. Naturally the two cops denied the arrest was a sham. But then why did Capone hand them a roll of bills along with his gun?

Why pay to get arrested? It sounds crazy but like his old boss Johnny Torrio, Al figured that prison was the safest port in a storm. After the St. Valentine's day shootings, things were sticky for a while. Bugs Moran was in hiding but might still pose a problem. Al decided it was safest to lie low for a while. His crime was only a minor one but the judge wasn't feeling sympathetic. Al expected a few months in **the cooler** – instead he got a sentence of a whole year. He was disgusted. He'd paid out good money for this arrest!

It must have been tough for the world's greatest gangster to put up with prison life.

AL'S SECRET DIARY

EASTERN PRISON, DECEMBER 15, 1929

Seven months now in this hellhole. Prison's a mean business and you gotta be tough to survive. Lucky I got ~~a~~ a cell to myself. (You expect me to share with criminals?)

I do my best to make the joint livable. Pity I ain't got much. Just my rugs and pictures, my chest of drawers, my bookshelf, books, and a few lamps. The radio set cost a bundle but it's worth it so's I can catch the baseball games. It's tough not having no telephone, but the Warden lets me use his anytime I want. After lunch they make us work. The job I

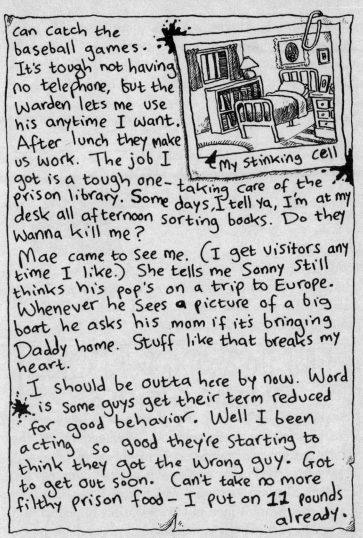

← My stinking cell

got is a tough one - taking care of the prison library. Some days, I tell ya, I'm at my desk all afternoon sorting books. Do they Wanna kill me?

Mae came to see me. (I get visitors any time I like.) She tells me Sonny still thinks his pop's on a trip to Europe. Whenever he sees a picture of a big boat he asks his mom if it's bringing Daddy home. Stuff like that breaks my heart.

I should be outta here by now. Word is some guys get their term reduced for good behavior. Well I been acting so good they're starting to think they got the wrong guy. Got to get out soon. Can't take no more filthy prison food - I put on 11 pounds already.

In the end Al got his sentence reduced to ten months. He'd been a model prisoner. As the prison doctor said: "I have never met a prisoner so kind, so cheerful and accommodating. I can't believe what they say about him."

While inside Al bought $1,000 of arts and crafts made by his prison inmates and sent them to his pals as Christmas presents. It was a good joke when you think about it – a big crook buying gifts made by crooks to hand out to other crooks.

When he finally got out of prison, the world had changed. Up to now Al had been known as Scarface or plain Al Brown. Now he found he'd got a new title. He was Public Enemy Number One.

THE LOWDOWN ON...
PUBLIC ENEMIES

The idea of Public Enemies was dreamed up by the Chicago Crime Commission. This body of Chicago's bigwigs had the brainwave of publishing a Gangsters Top Ten (actually it was a top 28, which wasn't so catchy). By listing the meanest men in Chicago, they hoped to turn the public against them. Surprisingly it worked. If you call someone a public enemy often enough, people will start to believe you (look at traffic wardens).

Here's the official Top Ten Public Enemies of 1930. You might have heard some of their names before.

THE TOP TEN - 1930

NO.1 AL "SCARFACE" CAPONE — STILL ON TOP OF THE COPS

NO.2 RALPH "BOTTLES" CAPONE — AL'S SOUL BROTHER

NO.3 FRANK RIO — BOOGIE ON WITH AL'S PERSONAL BODYGUARD

NO.4 "MACHINE GUN" JACK McGURN — TRIGGER-HAPPY HOOD WITH A STRING OF HITS

NO.5 "GREASY THUMB" GUZIK — AL'S MONEY MAN, STILL DOING THE FUNKY DOLLAR

NO.6 "BUGS" MORAN — CREEPY, CRAWLY, AND HALF CRAZY

NO.7 JOEY AIELLO — GUNNING FOR THE NO.1 SPOT

NO.8 SPIKE O'DONNELL — HAS BEEN WHO'S STILL MEAN

NO.9 "POLACK" JOE SALTIS — SOUTH SIDE SONGSTER MAKING A REAL RACKET

NO.10 MYLES O'DONNELL — HALF OF HIT DUO WITH BROTHER KLONDIKE

These were Chicago's most wanted criminals. Al must have been proud to see that the Capone band occupied the top five places. But it's a pity the Crime Commission didn't cast their net wider. Lower down

135

the list they could have included other gangsters who *deserved* to be famous. Not because they were bigshots in the underworld, but because they had such wonderfully nutty names. As you know, a gangster without a nickname was a nobody. Some nicknames, like "Scarface," were invented by the newspapers to liven up their crime pages. Other nicknames stuck to crooks because of some event in their past.

To set the record straight here's a few of America's more colorful gangsters who didn't make it on to the Public Enemies top-ten list.

1 Murray "the Camel" Humphreys

Probably the only Welsh gangster in America. Called the camel because of his surname – Hump-phreys (geddit?).

2 Sam "Golf Bag" Hunt

One of Al's gang. Once arrested for carrying a shotgun in his golf bag. (Cops eventually started to suspect that people carrying violin cases might not be musicians.)

3 "The Cavalier" (*Il Cavaliere*)

The Cavalier was Joseph Nerone, a Sicilian who earned his nickname because he walked and talked like an aristocrat. In fact Nerone wasn't a duke. Before becoming a gangster he'd been something much more sinister – a math teacher.

4 "Peg-leg" Lonergan

Brooklyn gangleader who lost his right leg in a railroad accident. Lots of hoods were in the habit of losing body parts (every job has its drawbacks). Peg-leg's gang included "Glass-eye" Pelicano, who was no relation to "Nine-toed" Nabors, or Willie "Three Fingers" White, a Capone gangster who could only count up to eight.

Call Me Number One

What was Al's reaction to being named Public Enemy Number One? Perhaps at first he was flattered.

But the title soon proved a heavy burden to carry. Almost every paper in America carried the Public Enemy list on its front pages. Now everybody knew who Al Capone was. He was no longer a daredevil outlaw. He was Public Enemy Number One.

AL'S SECRET DIARY

June 20, 1930

This Public Enemy stuff is driving me bananas. Al Capone gets the blame for everything. If there are no jobs, it's Al's fault. If some **doll*** gets robbed in the street, who's to blame? Al's the guy! If Al stays in, he's cooking up some deal. If he goes out, he's a danger to the public. I belch in a restaurant and half the customers dive for cover. I got a cop following me like a dog every time I leave the house. I can't go to the bathroom without this guy! And for what? Because my name's Al Capone - that's what!

Well, I ain't taking it no longer. They made me the goat for too long. Why pick on me? It ain't fair! Al's an American citizen. He's got rights like the next guy. All I ever do is sell beer and whiskey to our top people. All I do is give people what they want. The **cops** and the **judges** - they're all in the racket same as me. Only difference, they pretend they're straight! Give me a hard-working crook any day. At least he's honest!

Crooked judges and dodgy mayors

For once, Al had a point. He was no angel, but then he didn't pretend to be one. What about the crooked cops, the crooked judges, and the reporters on the take? If anyone should know about them it was Al. After all he was paying them a fortune in bribes every week!

The most amazing example was Big Bill Thompson. (Remember him?) Although booze was against the law, Big Bill drank like a fish. That wasn't unusual, but he should have set an example. After all he was Mayor of Chicago! Big Bill made it no secret that he liked to drink. When he ran for election in 1927, his slogan was:

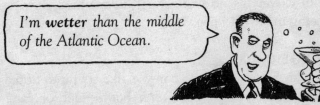

*I'm **wetter** than the middle of the Atlantic Ocean.*

An investigation later revealed that most of his campaign funds came from a certain Mr. A. Capone. Yet this was the man who claimed: "I drove the crooks out of Chicago and will do so again if I am elected Mayor."

Chicago judges were just as crooked as mayors. Once a police raid on the offices of Dr. A. Brown seized some valuable record books. Why were the police raiding a doctor's surgery? Because A. Brown was actually Al Capone and the medicine bottles on his shelf contained not pills but twenty types of booze. The record books were important evidence on Capone's shady dealings. So what did the Chicago judge handling the case do? He held a secret hearing and gave the records straight back to Capone!

Lower down the list, cops and reporters were just as crooked. In June 1930 a crime reporter called Jake Lingle was gunned down at the racetrack. The investigation that followed caused a scandal. It turned out Lingle was no ordinary reporter. On his $65 a week salary he lived like a prince, riding around in a chauffeured limousine. How did he do it? By operating as a secret go-between for the gangs and the police. The stink from the scandal was so bad the Chief of Police had to resign.

Crime in Chicago started with the mayor at City Hall and ran right down to the gangsters on the streets. Politicians, police, and crooks were working together hand-in-glove. It's no wonder Al complained that he was being made a scapegoat.

Straight cops

Finding an honest Chicago cop was like trying to find a straight banana in a fruit store, but sooner or later someone had to challenge Al Capone. That someone was a 26-year-old ex-college boy called Eliot Ness. Ness was the number-one enemy of Public Enemy Number One – if you follow. He made it his personal mission in life to nail Capone. Most people think it was Ness who finally sent Al to prison. In fact this is a load of bunk. The story was invented by none other than Eliot Ness. Years later (when he was broke) Ness wrote a book about his fight with Capone.[1] Being a modest sort of chap he naturally made himself the hero of the story. The truth is more surprising. More about that later, first Eliot the Hero.

1. Ness's book was called *The Untouchables*. Later it became a TV series and a major Hollywood film. But it was too late for poor Ness, he didn't live to see himself finally become a hero.

Eliot the Hero

Ness liked to see himself as the hero riding into town on a white horse to fight the bad guys. In fact Ness didn't have a white horse – he was just a Special Agent working for the U.S. Department of Justice. He was tall and handsome with striking blue eyes. His Norwegian parents named him after the English novelist George Eliot. This was a bit of a joke since George Eliot was actually a woman.

Eliot became a Special Agent because it sounded exciting and dangerous. Danger was Ness's middle name. Asked why he accepted the job of tackling Capone he said:

> *If you don't like action and excitement, you don't go into police work. And what the hell, nobody lives forever!*

Ness could see the Justice Department weren't winning the Prohibition war. It doesn't take a mathematical genius to see why. Take the situation in Chicago:

GOVERNMENT   VS.   CAPONE

300 AGENTS

1000 GANGSTERS

Who would you bet on? As if the war wasn't one-sided enough, Ness couldn't count on all his troops. Many of the Prohibition "dry" agents were actually "wet." This doesn't mean they were wilted greens, it means they were helping the bootleggers. Many of them beefed up their measly pay by taking bribes. It gave Ness a tricky problem. How could he hope to fight Capone when his own agents were as crooked as the enemy?

Ness solved the problem in true Hollywood tradition. What he needed was his own handpicked band of agents. They became known as . . .

The Untouchables

How did the Untouchables get their name? Have a guess. Was it . . .

a) Because they were very touchy about being touched?

b) Because they were extremely ticklish?

c) Because they couldn't be bribed?

You win an un-crooked banana if you said **c**. The Untouchables was a tag invented by the papers on hearing the news that Ness had (gasp!) turned down a bribe from Capone.

Ness knew his band of agents had to be out-of-the-ordinary. To be honest they had to be out of their minds. Why else would a few men take on a battle with an army of 1,000 thugs? To find his men, Ness started by making a list of the qualities he needed. If he'd placed an ad for the Untouchables, it might have looked something like this.

for further information. No experience necessary but must be able to start immediately.

WANTED – SPECIAL AGENTS

Must be single, under 30 years old and willing to work long hours for measly pay. Applicants should be handy with a gun and both fists. They should be skilled at tapping a telephone and expert at **tailing** an automobile (without looking as obvious as an ice-cream van).

Warning – if you take this job people will try to shoot you and blow you up. If that sounds exciting, you're the kind of weird and crazy guy I'm looking for.

In the end Ness whittled his shortlist down to nine men. These nine, together with Ness himself, became the rough, tough gangbusters known as the Untouchables.

YOU'RE CAUGHT!

THE ELIOT NESS MONSTER

The Untouchables looked a fearsome bunch but even Ness was nervous about the job they were taking on. Capone had had hundreds of men killed. How could Ness and his men succeed where everyone else had failed? In a way they didn't. It was someone else who put Capone behind bars.

Funster Frank Wilson

The man who nabbed Capone *wasn't* Eliot Ness. It was a hero of a different kind. The kind of hero who wore a mean pair of specs and was a whiz at figures. A hero who dared to be bald, forty, and work in an office. His name was Frank J. Wilson.

If you met Funster Frank at a party, you'd have thought he looked like a tax man.

That's because he *was* a tax man.

This was the man who'd finally nail Al Capone? Yes, the strange truth is that Al Capone was never jailed for murder or even for bootlegging. What got him in the end was not paying his taxes!

Al never gave the matter much thought.

How can you pay taxes on rackets that are against the law?

Wilson made it his mission to prove that Capone owed thousands of dollars in taxes. Since Al threw cash around like water, you'd think that would be so easy. But as one of Wilson's team said: "It was as easy as hanging a closed sign on the moon."

Al wasn't dumb. He never signed his name on contracts. When he bought a house or a saloon, he got someone else to do the deal. The truth was that, on paper, no one could prove that Al had a penny to his name.

145

Wilson's job was hard enough. But the government didn't make it any easier. They gave him just three assistants and an office the size of a broom closet.

I could hardly scratch my head without sticking my elbow in somebody else's eye.

You see, even tax men have a sense of humor!

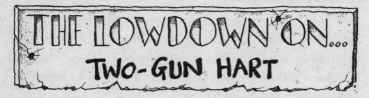

THE LOWDOWN ON...
TWO-GUN HART

Not all the Capone family were crooks. Al's older brother Vincenzo, who had vanished in 1905, ended up in another line of business. Strangely enough he was a Prohibition agent. While Al made a million from illegal booze, his brother arrested people in Nebraska for selling the stuff!

THERE'S ONE WHITE SHEEP IN EVERY FAMILY

Vincenzo changed his name to Hart to escape the famous Capone family name. But like his criminal brother, Hart was a bit of a show-off. He liked to dress as a cowboy with two pearl-handled pistols at his belt. He was a deadshot with a gun in either hand. One of his favorite tricks was to line up his three sons in a row. He placed cigarettes in their mouths and took careful aim. A second later – bang! bang! bang! The three cigarettes split in half and fell to the ground. His boys opened their eyes again and Dad gave them a pat on the head. He was still the best shot in the West.[1]

Time was running out for Al. The net was drawing tighter and tighter around him. Al had gotten rid of every mean hood in Chicago, but a team of **tax dicks** were to prove too clever for him. If only he'd paid his taxes!

1. WARNING – don't try this trick at home. If your Dad digs out his old cowboy boots – run!

GANGSTER SLANG

the cooler prison

doll 1920s slang for a babe!

floozie a woman with a bad reputation

dry agent prohibition agent supposed to enforce the liquor laws – in fact many of them sold liquor themselves to increase their wages!

wet someone who drinks or sells booze

tailing following a car

flivver a Ford car often used by the cops

dick detective

tax dick tax investigator

flatfoot cop

AL ON TRIAL

Spies, lies... and a nasty surprise

By 1929 the battle was well and truly on. The law versus Al Capone.

ELIOT "THE HERO" **NESS** & HIS UNTOUCHABLES v AL "SCARFACE" **CAPONE** & HIS GANGSTER ARMY

The battle plans were drawn up. Ness and his agents set out to smash Capone's empire, while Frank Wilson snooped quietly into Al's business affairs. Was Al worried? Are you kidding? He'd taken care of tougher enemies than this. Next to Crazy O'Banion or Hymie Weiss, Ness was just a bug in the ear. As for the tax investigation, Al never suspected a thing. Maybe he'd got too used to being Number One in Chicago. Or maybe he thought all the thousands he paid out in bribes would protect him. Either way, he didn't notice that his ship was sinking.

The war between Ness and Capone was a cat-and-mouse game. And for a change Al was cast as the mouse. The first round went to the Untouchables.

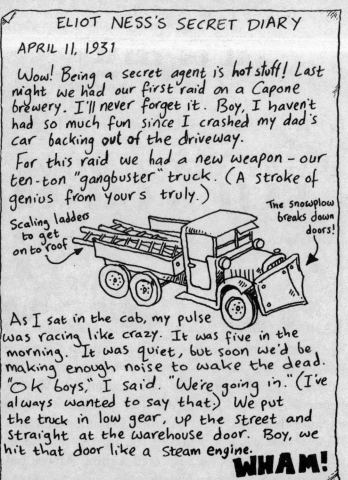

ELIOT NESS'S SECRET DIARY

APRIL 11, 1931

Wow! Being a secret agent is hot stuff! Last night we had our first raid on a Capone brewery. I'll never forget it. Boy, I haven't had so much fun since I crashed my dad's car backing out of the driveway.

For this raid we had a new weapon - our ten-ton "gangbuster" truck. (A stroke of genius from yours truly.)

Scaling ladders to get on to roof

The snowplow breaks down doors!

As I sat in the cab, my pulse was racing like crazy. It was five in the morning. It was quiet, but soon we'd be making enough noise to wake the dead. "Ok boys," I said. "We're going in." (I've always wanted to say that.) We put the truck in low gear, up the street and straight at the warehouse door. Boy, we hit that door like a steam engine. **WHAM!**

The snowplow ripped right through it like it was paper.

Inside Capone's boys were running like scared rabbits. Didn't know what hit 'em. You can bet they weren't expecting Eliot Ness to come busting through the door! I sure taught them a lesson.

We captured six men and two trucks. I guess we broke up brewery equipment worth near a $100,000. I made sure the press boys took plenty of pictures. (Especially of me arresting the six punks singlehanded.) I've ordered a dozen copies myself.

SAY CHEESE

me!

Modesty, as you know, wasn't one of Ness's many talents. He liked people to hear about his daring adventures. Just to make sure, he invited along reporters when he was going on a raid. The headlines the next day were all about the Untouchables and their latest victory. Ness tended to exaggerate his own importance. Nevertheless, Capone's gang decided he needed a warning. The very next day after the brewery raid, he got one.

NESS'S SECRET DIARY

April 12, 1931

Another exciting evening. Started out dull when I took my girlfriend Edna for a drive in the country. Things brightened up when I noticed a car was tailing us home!

I dropped Edna home and walked to my car. Just as I got in there was a bright flash from the windows. Lucky my razor-sharp instincts saved me. I ducked down just as my windshield was **shattered** by a bullet.

Without thinking I jammed my foot on the accelerator. As my car screeched away, another slug* shattered the window of my rear side-door.

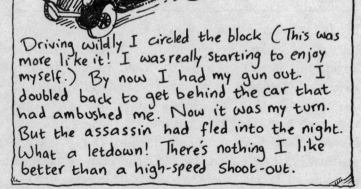

me!

Driving wildly I circled the block (This was more like it! I was really starting to enjoy myself.) By now I had my gun out. I doubled back to get behind the car that had ambushed me. Now it was my turn. But the assassin had fled into the night. What a letdown! There's nothing I like better than a high-speed shoot-out.

I had plenty to think about as I drove home. Someone is out to kill me. That sure makes me proud! Here I am, 26, with the deadliest mob in America out to get me. Can life get any more exciting than this? I can't wait to tell the boys about this tomorrow. Boy, will they be jealous!

Ness tried the same trick once too often. When he burst into the next Capone brewery, this is what he found.

You can imagine how dumb *that* made him look.

It hadn't taken Al long to get one step ahead of his enemy. If Ness could offer rewards for information, so could Al. And naturally the Big Guy's rewards were bigger. Anyone who knew the Untouchables were going on a raid could earn a cool $500 just by giving Capone the tip-off.

Meanwhile Al tried another old trick. If Ness couldn't be bumped off, then maybe he could be bought. Soon after, "the Kid" strolled into Ness's office. The Kid was a young boy who was one of Ness's informers. This

153

time he'd come with a message from Capone. He put a
large envelope on Ness's desk. When Ness looked
inside, he found a pair of thousand-dollar bills.

"They say that if you take it easy, you'll get the same
amount each and every week," said the Kid. Ness
angrily shoved the bribe back in the Kid's pocket.

> *I may only be a poor baker's son, but I don't need this
> kind of money. Now you go back and tell those rats what
> I said – and be damn sure you give them back every penny
> or so help me, I'll break you in half.*

At least that's the way Ness put it in his book. In real life
he probably wasn't so eloquent. When he left work that
day, the treasury agent suffered the final insult. His car had
been stolen. No prizes for guessing who was responsible.

> CAR? WHAT CAR?

Ness and his hit squad kept up the raids all year. And
they paid off. By 1932 the Untouchables had cost

Capone millions of dollars. They'd closed down breweries, dumped thousands of gallons of beer, and seized many of Capone's delivery trucks.

Ness even had the nerve to parade the trucks past Al's rooms at the Lexington Hotel. If it was meant to put the Big Boy's big nose out of joint, it worked. Al was so mad, he broke a chair in half.

Spies and disguise

Ness billed himself as the star of the show. But he wasn't the only one who was taking risks. Remember tax man Funster Frank Wilson? He'd spent two years trying to find papers that would prove Al's million-dollar income. But Wilson had drawn a blank and was on the point of giving up. The breakthrough came from a brainwave. What if an undercover agent joined Capone's gang? That way Wilson would get inside information on everything his enemy did. The agent chosen for this dangerous job was Mike Malone. (Eliot Ness would have been spotted as easily as an elephant in dark glasses.) Malone was small, with jet-black hair and a winning smile. He could easily pass for an Italian or Greek. But could he pass for a gangster? His life depended on it.

Malone sent back secret reports to Wilson. Maybe they read something like this.

TOP SECRET

Subject: Al Capone
Date: August 12, 1930
Agent: Mike Malone
Alias: Mike De Angelo

I'm in! It wasn't easy, but I'm now a paid-up member of Capone's mob. For a week I hung around the bar in the Lexington. I wore flashy suits, big rings, read the papers. I figured I looked the part. The question was, would Capone's boys buy it?

One night they took the bait. One of the mob spoke to me in the elevator. "We want **the McCoy** about you," he drawled. "You look like maybe you're **on the lam** and might be open to a proposition."

I played along. "Matter of fact, I am open for something, but it's gotta be good. If you want it straight, why I come here in the first place is I figured maybe I could tie in with the Big Boy."

The mobster said they'd have to do some checking on me. I waited a few days hoping my cover would hold. If it didn't, I knew I'd be taking a one-way trip. Soon after I got an invite to a party thrown by Capone himself. I'd heard all about Scarface's parties. He's the kind of guy who wines and dines a guest, then knocks them off with a baseball bat after dinner. Maybe that's what he had in mind for me. You can bet I didn't sleep too good the night before.

Scarface was at the party in a tux and bow tie. In the flesh he's impressive. Ice-cool eyes that take you in. For a moment I thought he'd mumbled I was a **spook**. Then he took out his fat hand and patted me on the shoulder.

"How ya doin' Mike? My boys tell me you're looking for a job."

I start today as a croupier dealing poker in one of Capone's gambling joints. I'll keep my head down and my ears open.

Malone was soon able to send his boss vital information. One morning he heard two Capone hoods mention someone they were "taking care of." The target was staying at the Sherman Hotel. Malone realized it was his own boss, Frank Wilson! Taking a huge risk, he phoned Wilson at his hotel room and told him to get out fast. The message saved Wilson's life. That night his body would have been dumped in the river with a weight tied to his feet.

Soon after another agent called Graziano joined Malone. It was Graziano who stumbled on the vital evidence to bring down Al Capone.

TOP SECRET

Subject: Al Capone
Date: October 4, 1930
Agent: Graziano

My job is checking on Capone's beer deliveries. Yesterday I got talking to one of Capone's boys about a raid some years back on the Hawthorn Tobacco Shop. The hoodlum was boasting and having a laugh at our expense. He said: "The income tax dicks ain't so smart. They walked out with a little accounting book from the tobacco shop that could've sent the Big Boy to jail, only they're too dumb to realize it." I couldn't get any more without sticking my nose in too far. It's probably nothing, does it mean anything to you?

Did it mean anything? For two years Wilson had been trying to find proof that Capone made money. Now he realized that he had the proof all the time! He ransacked his office for days looking for a "little accounting book." Finally – just as he was about to give up – he found it. There were three black books showing profits from the Big Boy's gambling rackets. As soon as Wilson saw them, he knew judgment day had dawned for Al Capone.

Big-hearted Al

Al had his back to the wall. It was only a matter of time before he'd have to stand trial. What could he do? In typical Al fashion he decided the answer to his problems was popularity. Since St. Valentine's Day, Al's public image had taken a nosedive. But Al knew money could buy a lot of things and popularity was one of them. This was the 1930s and there were millons of people who needed a handout. Chicago was no longer the boom town of the 1920s. Like the rest of America it had been rocked by the Great Depression.

The 1920s are known to history as the "Roaring Twenties." What came next was more like the Groaning Thirties. The twenties were a boom time. It was the age of jazz, wild living, and making scads of money (look at Al Capone).

Most Americans thought it would go on forever. Many of them put their life savings into the stock market. (Which is like betting your entire piggy bank on a horse. Risky.) Even banks took big risks with their money in the craze to make profits. Something was bound to happen. And on Black Thursday, October 24, 1929, it did. Millions of people's savings were wiped out as shares sank like a stone. In one day the New York Stock market lost 4 BILLION dollars. Black Thursday was the start of the Great Depression.

It was a period of terrible poverty. By 1932:

- one in four Americans was out of work
- 10,000 banks had gone bust
- farm prices had fallen by over a half since 1929.

Poor farmers were thrown out of their homes and lands. They fled west in scrap-heap trucks searching for work, only to find jobs didn't exist. Ramshackle slums called Hoovervilles (after President Herbert Hoover) grew up on the edge of every city.

Chicago was one of the worst hit. Just when the city needed money, they found most of it had gone. Where? Into the pockets of the city's noble mayor, where else? Big Bill Thompson had a lot of expenses (whiskey, beer, brandy, etc.) so he'd helped himself out of people's taxes. Even the gangsters were having a tough time of it. People were too poor to buy bootleg beer and whiskey. They were more interested in bread to fill their empty bellies.

In a time of national disaster, who could help the poor and hungry of Chicago?

JUST CALL ME SANTA CLAUS!

PRESENTS

Big-hearted Al had cash in his sack and he wanted to share it. He opened a soup kitchen in Chicago and fed 5,000 people a day. It was a grand gesture and won Al a lot of friends among the poor.

Of course it wasn't out of pure kindness. Al thought that if the public loved him, he wouldn't get sent to prison.

As his trial approached Al milked his big-hearted image for all it was worth. If he'd wanted a character reference, he could have found lots of fans.

Here are just two of the letters that might have been written. (The stories are true.)

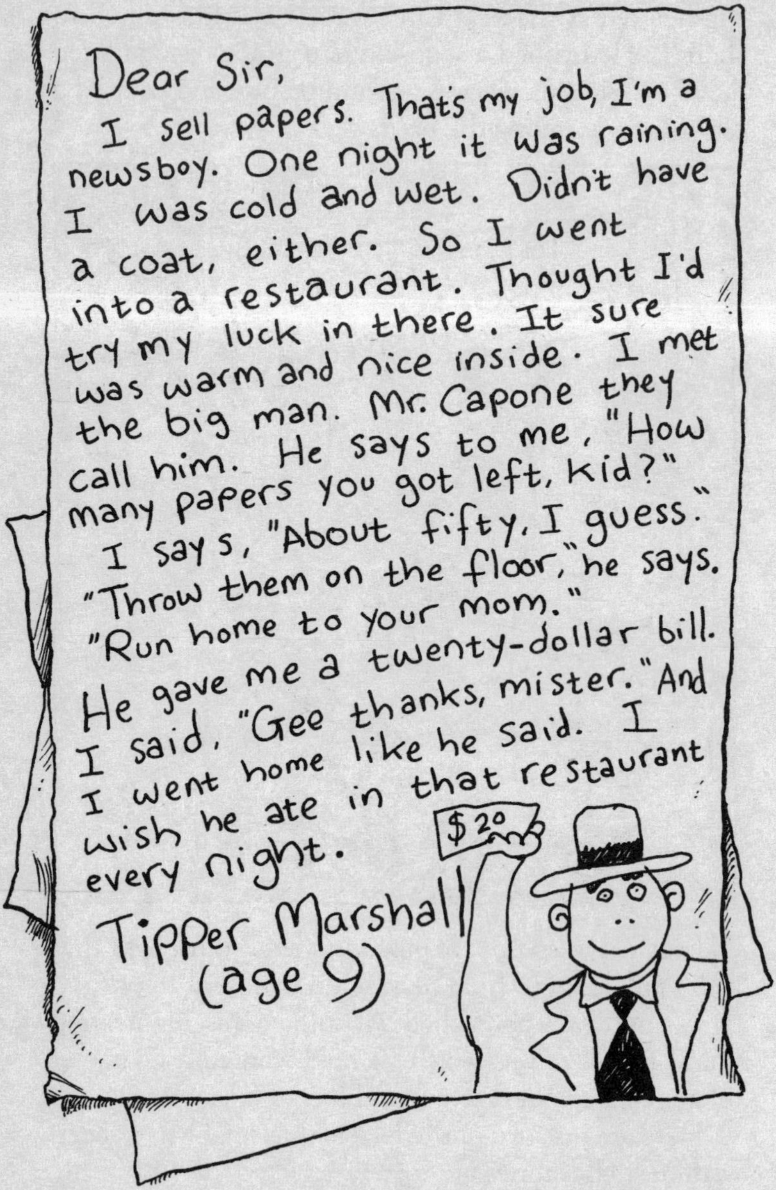

Dear Sir,

I sell papers. That's my job, I'm a newsboy. One night it was raining. I was cold and wet. Didn't have a coat, either. So I went into a restaurant. Thought I'd try my luck in there. It sure was warm and nice inside. I met the big man. Mr. Capone they call him. He says to me, "How many papers you got left, kid?"

I says, "About fifty, I guess."
"Throw them on the floor," he says. "Run home to your mom."

He gave me a twenty-dollar bill. I said, "Gee thanks, mister." And I went home like he said. I wish he ate in that restaurant every night.

Tipper Marshall (age 9)

Dear Sir,

I'm a singer. Harry Richman's the name. One night Al Capone came to see me perform. I don't mind telling you I was shaking like a leaf. After the show he came to my dressing room and grabbed me in a bear hug. "Richman, you're the greatest!" he boomed.

Sometimes it amuses me to carry a few $1,000 bills. I wave them around in restaurants to impress the waiters. Then I started to get held up in the street. Every time I left the theater, some **roughneck** would jump out and point a gun at me. It was a nightmare. So I told Mr. Capone my problem. "I'll fix that," he said.

He took me for a drive. When we got back to his office, a package was waiting for me. "There's your stuff," said Capone. I tore it open and there was my jewelry and my $1,000 bills. It was like magic. Capone snapped his fingers and it was done! I tried to thank him but he wouldn't hear of it.

"Forget it, kid," he said. "You're a great entertainer. I love ya like a kid brother." That was the mark of Al Capone. Incredible generosity – and such power!

Harry Richman (Vaudeville Star)

Hundreds of tales could truely be told about Al's generosity.

Of course Al knew these stories didn't do his image any harm. He had a simple message for the public. He wasn't a thug or a gorilla, he was a nice guy. It was true Al had a big heart. More to the point, he had a big check book. But when it came to his trial could these things help him? Al thought so. He wasn't worried about his court case. After all, he'd faced plenty of charges before. And he'd spent a lot of time working on his defense. In Al's book, of course, that meant one thing – cheating.

AL'S SECRET DIARY June 2, 1931

So the tax dicks think they can send Al for a long stretch* in the slammer*? They can think again. Al's been inside once and he ain't planning to go back in a hurry. I've drawn up a plan with my lawyers to get me off the hook. It's pretty smart, if I say so myself.

1. Send the boys around to pay these tax spooks a visit. See how they like it when the heat's on them.

2. Find out the names of the jury. Offer them a square deal - a little dough for them, a little sentence for me - everybody's happy.

3. If all else fails, cut a deal with the prosecution. A million bucks oughta do it. I ain't trying to bribe no one, I just figure they could use a little help to reach the right decision.

The right decision for me, that is.

This time all Al's tricks were in vain. He was left with no choice but to face the music.

THE CHICAGO BUGLE

July 30, 1931

JUDGE SAYS 'NO DEAL FOR CAPONE'

The Capone case took a sensational twist today when the judge said that justice could not be bought. This was obviously news to Al Capone. In the past he's bribed his way out of every tight corner. He looked stunned and speechless.

Chicago's crime-king had looked confident as he swaggered into court. He was wearing a pea-green suit topped by a white fedora. Capone had pleaded guilty in return for a light sentence. His lawyer, Albert Fink said, "We understood a deal had been struck. If our client pleaded guilty, he'd get a token sentence. Two or three years tops. The judge's attitude is shocking. Anyone would think he doesn't want to help Al!"

Judge Wilkerson made it clear he was cutting no deals. An angry Wilkerson told the court: "It's time for somebody to teach the defendant that it's utterly impossible to bargain with the court."

Maybe Capone is at last going to be made to pay for his crimes. The people of Chicago have had a bellyful of his tricks. It's time for him to face the music. The case opens on October 6. It promises to be the trial of the century.

The King of Cool

During his trial the newspapers were impressed with Al's clothes. Whenever he was in the spotlight the Big Guy always liked to look his best.

On the opening day of his trial Al dressed quietly (for him).

On each day of the trial Al put on a suit of a different color. Purple, green, yellow – Al never wore the same clothes two days running and always looked as cool as a cucumber. The fortune he spent on fashion even became part of the case. At one point a shop salesman told the court that Al wore Italian silk underwear. Spectators giggled and Al blushed to his fingertips. Chicago's crime king wasn't used to having his undies discussed in public!

Even as the trial began Al thought he could get off the hook. After all, he'd paid for the best lawyers and he still had one trick up his sleeve. The jury had been bribed with cash, boxing tickets, or anything they wanted. They couldn't find Al guilty, could they?

If we could read Al's secret diaries during the trial, we'd discover that Mr. Cool was soon sweating.

AL'S SECRET DIARY
Tuesday, October 6, 1931   (First day in court)

Hot! Crowded! Cops everywhere. (It takes 40 of them just to escort me into court. Boy are they nervous!) The courtroom's jammed with reporters and rubbernecks* come to see the show.

Things are going well until the jury are called. Fink, my lawyer, turns pale. They ain't on any of our lists! You know the trouble my boys've been to paying off these guys? I figure we can come to some arrangement that'll suit everybody. And what happens? The judge goes and switches the jury with another court! Is that playing fair? Is that justice? Damn right it ain't!

Thursday, October 8, 1931

Call my tailor over to the Lexington. Gotta have a couple of new suits for the trial. A man of my standing's gotta think of his public. **NO ONE'S** gonna Say Al looked like a **BUM** in court. While I'm getting measured, Frankie Rio plays the wise guy. "You don't need to be ordering no fancy duds,*" he cracks.

"You're going to prison. Why don't you have a suit made with stripes on it?"

"The hell I am!" I tell him. "I'm going to Florida for a nice long rest. You wait and see."

Friday, October 9, 1931

They start in about Florida today. How Al pays for his joint on Palm Island, the boats, the Swimming Pool, the parties, the whole works. They pull in the manager of the Western bank to rat on me. But Whadd'ya know? The poor Sap's lost his memory. Ain't that a crying shame? They keep on with the questions but he just don't recall who sent them money orders from Chicago. Maybe it's amnesia. Anyone can get forgetful. Especially when one of my boys is sitting in the front row with a gun under his coat.

um er

Thursday, October 15, 1931

Only two more days. I figure we got them on the ropes but it ain't easy to call. Today they call Oscar Guttie to the stand. Oscar's a bookie. He tells how I lose 60,000 bucks on the ponies in one year. Sixty big ones and they expect Al to be paying taxes. Truth is they ought to be paying me!

Saturday, October 17, 1931

We're down to the wire. Fink gets first shot at summing up the case for the jury. He puts it to them straight. Al ain't no piker* He ain't the kind of guy to cheat the government. Al's the kind of guy who never fails a friend. That sure chokes me up. My eyes are watering so bad I gotta reach for my hanky.

That big creep Johnson starts in for the prosecution next. The way he tells it Al never did nothing for no one but himself. **I'D LIKE TO SLUG THAT GUY IN THE PUSS!** So what if I buy a few dozen silk shirts? So what if I spend a few bucks on diamond belt buckles. Ain't a guy got the right to dress nice? Nobody puts his hand deeper in his pocket than Al Capone. Know what? They oughta put a statue of me outside City Hall.

2:40 p.m. The jury files out. They ain't looking me in the eye. Maybe it ain't looking so good.

10 p.m. Still no word. The waiting is driving me crazy. What's taking them so long? You only gotta look at me to tell I'm innocent!

When the jury finally returned, Al heard the words he'd been dreading.

The judge gave Al Capone an 11-year sentence. All through the trial the Big Guy had smiled for his public. Now the smile finally drained away. Eleven years! He'd been expecting three at the worst. It was the longest sentence that had ever been handed out for tax evasion.

In the end it was Al's fame that brought about his own downfall. He wasn't sentenced just for tax dodging. He got 11 years because the judge and jury knew he was the biggest gangster, bootlegger, and murderer in Chicago. "It blew me away," muttered Al. "But what can you expect when the whole community is prejudiced against you?"

GANGSTER SLANG

slug a bullet (but if you slugged a guy, you punched him)

the McCoy the genuine article, the truth (named after a rum-runner called McCoy who smuggled good liquor)

REAL McCOY FAKE McCOY

on the lam in hiding

spook a spy

roughneck a thug

stretch prison sentence

the slammer jail

rubberneck a person who gawks and stares

fancy duds smart clothes

piker a mean, miserly, tight, and stingy person

sugar money (don't ask a gangster for sugar in your tea)

CONVICT CAPONE

Prisons, pelicans, and going crazy

The last time Al had been sent to prison, he'd lived a life of luxury. This time things would be different. He was no longer Al Capone, big-shot crime king. Behind bars he was just prisoner number 40822.

PRISONER NO. 40822

CRIME: Income tax evasion
SENTENCE: 11 years
AGE: 33
OCCUPATION: Gambler, racketeer, bootlegger . . . take your pick

As soon as Al arrived at the Atlanta jail, he was fingerprinted and photographed. His clothes were taken away and he got a prison haircut (in other words a scalping).

Al only spent the first two years of his sentence in the Atlanta Jail. He didn't realize but this was the cushy part. Much worse was to come. No doubt Al would've recorded his feelings about "doing time" in his secret diary.

AL'S SECRET DIARY
May 28, 1932

Back in the cooler again. Boy it stinks! Imagine! Some creep gets Al Capone on a damn tax rap and Al ends up cooling his heels for 11 years. **11 Years**! Ain't that a helluva deal? How's a fella gonna stick it without **losing his marbles*** ? The boys here gave me a big reception. Banging on the bars of their cells and cheering like crazy. You'da thought the heavyweight champ of the world was arriving. I guess even in a lousy hole like this I'm pretty famous.

They throw me in a cell with eight other guys. How d'ya like that? Do they know who I am? Luckily one of my cellmates is an old pal of mine. Rusty Rudensky- one of the best **mechanics*** in the business. Boy am I glad to see his ugly mug!

I soon get Rusty doing a few jobs for me. Prison ain't no different from anywhere else. If you got the cash, you can grease a few wheels. Rusty keeps my "bank" inside a hollow broom handle. Comes in handy. Yesterday a couple of dumb hillbillies thought they'd take a shot at Al Capone. They jumped me during chow time* and roughed me up a little. Next day the two jackasses got theirs in spades.* The way I hear it, they'll be in the hospital for quite a few weeks. Al may be in the cooler but he's still the Big Guy.

Al's money talked inside prison just as it had in Chicago. He had a beefy team of bodyguards who followed him everywhere. During recreation, if Al wanted a game of tennis he just pointed to the convict he wanted to play. That was the signal for the other player on the court to hand over his racket and make a quick exit. When it came to baseball, Al thought he was a natural.

I'm a pretty good pitcher and first baseman, though I do say so myself.

Unfortunately no one else agreed. The pudgy gangster couldn't get into the prison baseball team, not even for a fat bribe!

All in all, Al's life in the Atlanta prison was bearable. But it didn't last. The government had just built a new super-prison to house the toughest criminals – the kidnappers, murderers, and gangsters – like Capone. In August 1934 Al got a transfer to the new jail. It was a place he'd never forget.

Welcome to Alcatraz

> *Alcatraz is a jail of eternal silence. No prisoner may speak except during one authorized period a week from one to three-thirty on Saturday. It's enough to drive you crazy.*

That's how an inmate described the prison in 1935. Imagine it. Six days a week of total, utter silence. And it wasn't just the silence, it was the harsh discipline, the vicious punishments, and the certainty that you would never, ever escape. Alcatraz was set on an island a mile and a half from San Francisco. Its Spanish name meant the Island of Pelicans. It was more like the Island of the Doomed. If you were planning escape, this is what you were up against.

Doing time

During Al's stay, five prisoners once tried to make a break for it. One was killed, one wounded, and one re-captured before they could get off the island. The other two were never found dead or alive. They probably drowned in the ice-cold sea and the swirling fog.

The man running the prison was Warden James A. Johnson. Prisoners called him "Pussy-foot" Johnson as a grim joke. In fact Johnson was as gentle as a tiger with a toothache. From the start he was determined prisoner number 85 would get no favors. Al got a cell to himself – but it wasn't exactly the Ritz. His room measured less than 10 feet by 5 feet – hardly room to swing a cat even if you had one (which rules didn't allow). Besides his bunk bed, Al's only furniture was a folding table, a tin sink, and a toilet. The toilet didn't have a seat because the warden didn't want prisoners getting too comfy.

MAIN ENTRANCE-3 DOOR SECURITY SYSTEM

MESS HALL KNOWN AS THE GAS CHAMBER. TEAR GAS CAN BE RELEASED FROM THE CEILING IN CASE OF TROUBLE

CELL BLOCKS – PAINTED PINK AND WHITE TO MAKE THEM CHEERFUL!

ONE AND A HALF MILES TO SAN FRANCISCO LANDING DOCK

There was no privacy either – when you sat on your toilet, you could see another **con** across the way going about his business.

One day in silent, gloomy Alcatraz was like any other. It was no wonder that the routine drove many of the prisoners crazy. No prisoners were allowed to wear watches. Their lives were controlled by bells.

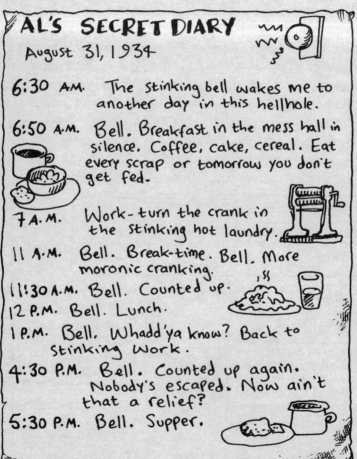

AL'S SECRET DIARY
August 31, 1934

6:30 A.M. The stinking bell wakes me to another day in this hellhole.

6:50 A.M. Bell. Breakfast in the mess hall in silence. Coffee, cake, cereal. Eat every scrap or tomorrow you don't get fed.

7 A.M. Work- turn the crank in the stinking hot laundry.

11 A.M. Bell. Break-time. Bell. More moronic cranking.

11:30 A.M. Bell. Counted up.

12 P.M. Bell. Lunch.

1 P.M. Bell. Whadd'ya know? Back to stinking work.

4:30 P.M. Bell. Counted up again. Nobody's escaped. Now ain't that a relief?

5:30 P.M. Bell. Supper.

> 6 P.M. Bell. Back to stinking cell blocks to be counted (again!)
>
> 6:30 P.M. Bell. Lock-up. No newspapers, no radio, no talking. Al lays on his bunk and wishes he was anywhere but in this lousy bughouse.
>
> 9:30 P.M. Bell. Lights out. Another day over. Only 3,001 more to go.

Play it again, Al

Saturdays and Sundays were fun days in Alcatraz. Prisoners got a break from the routine for two whole hours in the afternoon. As a further treat they were actually allowed to speak. After all that drudgery, you can imagine the thrilling conversations.

To get him through the long dark days Al turned to his old love – music. He couldn't go to the opera or listen to jazz, but he could do the next best thing. He could play in a band. Of course there were a couple of problems. First, Alcatraz didn't have a band and second, Al couldn't play a note. That didn't stop him. He went to Warden Johnston with his idea. He even offered to buy instruments for the inmates himself. Clarinets, trombones, trumpets, double bass – money was no object, he had plenty. Warden Johnson considered the idea for two seconds and then gave his usual answer . . . No.

Al didn't give up easily. He kept on asking for a year until finally he got his way. The band was allowed to practice for 20 minutes a day – providing each prisoner bought his own instrument. The Alcatraz combo weren't the best band in the business, but they were certainly the deadliest.

For a while all went well. But asking criminals to play in harmony was asking for trouble. Sooner or later someone was bound to hit a bad note. It was Al who did it. Not satisified with playing the banjo, he bought himself a mandolin. This made the rest of the band green with envy. They whispered that Al's mandolin had cost him a cool $600.

Soon after, a fight broke out at a practice session. It started with Al swearing at Harmon Waley for blowing his saxophone right in his ear. The young kidnapper waited till Al turned his back, then "accidentally" whacked Al on the head with his sax. In seconds the two prisoners were rolling around on the floor punching each other. It marked the end of Al's band practice. From then on he was forced to pursue a solo career.

APPARENTLY THEY'RE SPLITTING BECAUSE OF ARTISTIC DIFFERENCES

The horrible Hole

As you know, Warden Johnston wasn't fond of criminals. He believed the only way to deal with them was to break them. The thought of turning bad men to good never crossed his mind. Why waste your time on common crooks?

At night he ordered the guards to hold shooting practice in the prison yard. Their targets were man-shaped dummies. The next morning the bullet-riddled dummies were left out as a warning. Anyone thinking of escape had better think again. The guards weren't supposed to beat the prisoners. But if an inmate made trouble, what could they do? There were other punishments, too:

The horrible Hole was the torture chamber of Alcatraz. Instead of racks and hot coals, Johnson dreamed up something worse. THE DARK. Once the steel door slammed shut, the victim was in total darkness. The tiny room had nothing but a mattress and a hole in the floor for a toilet. Imagine it – 24 hours a day, seven days a week, crying and gibbering alone in the pitch black. The only meals were bread and water pushed through a slit in the door.

Breaking a prison rule carried a punishment of three days in the Hole. Attacking a prison guard could lead to weeks of the torture. Nineteen days was reckoned to be the most any prisoner could stand. Yet one convict who attacked Capone was shut in the horrible Hole for *six months*! Not surprisingly he went nuts.

Alcatraz soon had more nut-cases than a squirrel. The mind-numbing routine and the regular stays in the Hole sent many a prisoner stark raving mad. One inmate screamed whenever a plane flew over the island. Another convict walked around with his head wrapped in towels.

He wasn't washing his hair, he was protecting himself from "invisible tormentors." Prisoner number 284, Rube Persfal, went even further. One morning he took an ax and chopped off all the fingers on his left hand while laughing like a hyena. He begged a guard to chop off his right hand before he was dragged away to the hospital. No one ever heard of him again.

Crazy Capone

In this island of madmen how was prisoner number 85 getting along? After a year in Alcatraz, a marked change had come over Capone. He was a shadow of his former swaggering self.

The truth was that Al Capone was slowly going crazy. He wandered around in a daze, singing softly and talking to himself.

If you could glance at his secret diary in 1935, you'd soon have noticed the change.

AL'S SECRET DIARY June 4 1935

Another lousy night. I ain't sleeping so good. Who can sleep in a lousy joint like this? The screws* walk up and down all night, their boot leather squeaking on the floor. The foghorns hoot in the bay. Guys bawl and holler in their coops. It's a nut farm,* I tell ya. Just when they think I'm asleep, Dion walks in and sits down on my bunk. Remember Barmy O'Banion, the flower seller? I went to his funeral.

"How ya doing, Dion?" I ask.

"Not so good, Al" he says, and shows me the bullet holes in his chest.

"That's too bad," I say. "Who pulled the roscoe* on ya?"

"You did, Al," he laughs. (Fact is, I think he's kinda nuts.) Next thing he starts floating up to the ceiling. He waves to me, "Come on, Al, we're bustin' outta here!" and floats right through the bars of the cell. I can hear his laugh echoing all the way down the passageways. I swear to God that guy's a real loony tune!!

Life in the slow lane

What was happening to Al was worse than **stir bugs**. For a long time – without knowing – he'd suffered a serious brain disease. It's possible this was what caused Al's violent fits of temper all his life. By this stage the disease was affecting his nervous system. Al's speech was slurred and his movements were slow. Sometimes he was clear-headed and other times mixed up and confused.

Soon everyone knew there was something wrong with the Big Guy. One day there was a traffic jam in the lunch line. The hold-up was Al Capone. In a daze he let people pass him by. Shuffling along at the back of the line, he staggered and threw up on the dining room floor. It was a pathetic sight. The man who'd once run the city of Chicago, was led away to the prison hospital like a helpless baby.

Capone never recovered. He spent the rest of his sentence in the hospital. Crazy cases like him were cooped up in wire "bug cages." Al's neighbor across the ward was a crazy bank robber called Carl Janaway. The two spent their days yelling insults across at each other "like two six-year-olds in a sandbox." Once the row got so heated they reached for their bedpans like mad gunfighters. In seconds the air was filled with handfuls of poop flying across the ward.

TWO CAN PLAY AT THAT GAME!

The hospital staff kept back till the battle of the bedpans was over. Well, would you have stepped into the line of fire?

Al's potty behavior finally did what all his lawyers had failed to do. He was shipped out of Alcatraz. His last day on the Rock was January 6, 1939. His four years on the island of silence had reduced him to a ghost of his old self. Later that year he was finally released. Reporters asked "Greasy Thumb" Guzik if Capone would return to head the gang. The reply was simple.

Al is as nutty as a fruitcake.

Rotten retirement

Al spent his last years in his old Palm Island retreat where his family looked after him. He lived in his own world hardly even aware of outside events – like the little matter of World War Two.

In the past, the Miami villa had seen lavish parties, regular police visits and a stream of gangsters and reporters calling at the gates. Now it was as quiet as a retirement home. Al lived a ghostly existence. Sometimes he sat for hours on the dock with a fishing rod and a cigar. Sometimes he read the paper, especially if there was a story about him (not so often these days). Occasionally some of his pals dropped by for a game of cards. Once when Al lost, he threw the deck at the hood who'd dared to beat him.

"Who's this smart guy" he demanded. "Tell the boys to take care of him."

At one time the order would have been carried out. But not anymore.

Dead end

Finally, on January 25, 1947, Al breathed his last. His old mother, Sonny and his brothers and sisters were at his side. A crowd of reporters waited at the gate. Al would have been pleased, he always loved publicity. In the end Al didn't die the death of a gangster, riddled with bullets on the street. He died peacefully in his bed. He looked like a sweet, gray-haired old man in silk pajamas. You'd never have guessed he was only 48 years old.

Capone was buried in his old stomping ground in Chicago on a bitterly cold, snowy day. The millionaire gangster who had lived like a prince had the simplest of gravestones. Maybe no words could sum up a life like his.

Two-faced Capone

What can you say about Al Capone in the end? He is dead-famous as the greatest gangster in all history. A ruthless hoodlum who rose to the top of the pile by the force of his brains and brutality. But his family and his pals talked about a different Al Capone. Sonny said he hoped his dad would be remembered as: "a kind of outlaw like Jesse James, taking from the rich and giving to the poor."[1]

So which was the true Al Capone – the hero or the villain? Opinions were divided.

Al Capone: 1899–1947

Al Capone was a swaggering, big-hearted man who never turned his back on anyone. Al was rich as a king but he was no Scrooge. Who else would drive through the streets of Chicago scattering coins out the window? Crowds used to gather just to get a glimpse of the Big Fellow. How many poor folks would have frozen if it wasn't for Al giving them coal to get them through the winter? They couldn't blame him for being a bootlegger. As Al said himself, "if people didn't want beer, a guy would be crazy going around trying to sell it." Al was smart. He was the guy who brought business methods to the underworld. Say what you like about him, Al did what others only dream of. He was the poor kid who became a millionaire.

1. Sonny was getting his outlaws mixed up. It was Robin Hood who gave to the poor.

Scarface Capone: 1899–1947

Scarface Capone was the ugly face of mob rule in America. Other gangsters came and went but none could lick the Big Guy. Capone liked to pose as a respectable family man. But under the skin he was big headed, bad-tempered, and dangerous. No one knows how many men he killed or had "taken care of." If someone was in his way, Scarface had them bumped off. It wasn't revenge. It was just smart business. For all his charm and his style, no one should forget that Al Capone was a cold-blooded killer.

Which is the real Al Capone? The answer is both. Famous Dead characters are not always good *or* evil and Al was a puzzling mixture of both. The same man who ordered the deaths of seven men on St. Valentine's Day would, years later, open a soup kitchen to feed the poor. He was kind and cruel, generous and ruthless. Mae always believed he was a good man who the papers painted as evil. Al probably kidded himself in the same way. Before his tax trial he complained: "It's utterly impossible for a man of my age to have done all the things with which I am charged. I'm a spook born of a million minds."

That was Al Capone: gangster, legend, bogeyman – the man who *was* Chicago in the 1920s. He was a hero and a villain. A showman who always played to the gallery. One thing is certain – he made sure he'd never be forgotten. Forty years later Al still had one trick left up his sleeve . . .

THE CHICAGO BUGLE

April 23, 1986

CAPONE'S MISSING MILLIONS

It was billed as Chicago's answer to the tomb of Tutankhamen. Was this secret vault the lost treasure trove of Al Capone?

hidden under the hotel for the last forty years? Yesterday, while the TV cameras rolled and viewers watched breathlessly, the bulldozers moved in.

Was this Al's hiding place?

The vault was only recently discovered under the floor of the ruined Lexington Hotel. During the 1920s the Lexington was Capone's HQ from where he ran his multimillion-dollar crime empire. But until now Capone's missing millions have never been found. Had the loot been

Where's the lolly?

In his heyday Al Capone was said to be worth 25 million dollars. Yet when he died he claimed to be as poor as a church mouse. Was it true – or had he stashed the loot in some secret place? Reports say his wife and child never got the money. Mae and Sonny had to sell the house and for a while they ran a failing restaurant together.

They weren't the only ones with a claim to Al's money. When he died, Capone still owed the tax man over $200,000. A tax officer was there to watch the vault opened yesterday. "If there's any cash, I'm here to claim our share," said the hopeful revenue man.

All wall

But when the two-foot concrete wall was broken down it revealed . . . another wall. When that was demolished – the presenter of the TV show began to look desperate. "I don't know how to tell you this, but we've hit another wall," he told viewers. Finally the sealed vault was blasted open. When the dust settled, the secret of the vault was laid bare.

Apart from a few empty gin bottles, the vault was empty. The TV show fell flat. The tax man left empty-handed. Capone had fooled them again. Maybe somewhere down the corridors of the old hotel ghostly laughter echoed.

GANGSTER SLANG

losing your marbles
going crazy

mechanic a safe cracker

chow-time mealtime

in spades card game
slang – getting more than
you bargained for

con convict

screws prison guards

roscoe gun

stir bugs prison madness

coffin a cell

doghouse watchtower
on the prison wall

the warden's office a
prison toilet!

**nut farm, squirrel
college** hospital for
insane criminals

the bricks, the street
the world outside prison